A PRAEGER WORLD OF ART PROFILE

MATISSE

MATISSE

Jean Guichard-Meili

FREDERICK A. PRAEGER, Publishers
New York • Washington

BOOKS THAT MATTER

Published in the United States of America in 1967
by Frederick A. Praeger, Inc., Publishers
111 Fourth Avenue, New York, N. Y. 10003

© 1967, in Paris, by Fernand Hazan

Artistic rights © by s.p.a.d.e.m., Paris 1967

Library of Congress Catalog Card Number : 67-20401
Translated from the French by Caroline Moorehead

Printed in France

Contents

Foreword   7

CHAPTER ONE
Art in the 1890s   9

CHAPTER TWO
Life and Work   29

CHAPTER THREE
What is a Matisse?   125

CHAPTER FOUR
The World of Matisse   181

CHAPTER FIVE
After his Death   229

CHAPTER SIX
Collections and Books   235

List of Illustrations   245

Index   253

Foreword

Matisse died in 1954, at the age of eighty-five, in the midst of the things he was working on, his plans, his ceaselessly renewed creation. He had not failed his glory. This old man, ill for many years, but fully active and youthful in spirit, has become one of those beacons which, to take Baudelaire's metaphor, light up an entire era. The gods of art give to those whom they love a long life, productive up to their last days, except when they gather them up in their prime, like Raphael, Géricault or Seurat. For half a century the names of Matisse and Picasso will have been pronounced just as in other times those of Ingres and Delacroix, or Michelangelo and Leonardo, like symbols of two major tendencies which, from era to era, rule over painting: to subjugate the world, and to glorify it.

JEAN GUICHARD-MEILI

Henri - Matisse

1 Art in the 1890s

Sixty-two years of painting in a life span of eighty-five years are a long time. The resemblances between the last works of Matisse and his first attempts, correspond to the distance which separates the end of the nineteenth century and the middle of the twentieth. The patient perfecting of his spirit and the sure assertion of his art can be contrasted with the incoherent agitation of a universe racked by wars and revolutions, the giddiness of uncontrolled power and unsuccessful internal policy.

No man, however, is an island. No artist either, however great he is to become. At the critical moment when the dice, which decides his career, is thrown, he still owes everything to what he himself loves and chooses; his possibilities remain unknown, his future without contours. The moment of a new birth, self-conscious and anxious, comes at the threshold between his adolescence and his manhood. In three or four years he devours, accumulates or rejects; he fathoms out the past, questions the present, and judges. Once the obedience and passivity of school studies are put aside, the critical faculty asserts itself.

More no doubt than the country or the race, more too than the origins of the atmosphere of childhood, the circumstances surrounding this moment of truth in an artist's life, around his twentieth year, are worth examining closely.

Matisse was twenty at the beginning of 1890. He was almost twenty-three when he decided to follow his vocation, and to leave his home for Paris. At this time France was a rich and powerful country, believing in peace and not over-shadowed by fear. General Boulanger had not yet dared to attempt the adventure of personal power. The serious Sadi Carnot was President of the Republic. Since the French were not at that moment engaged in international conflicts all their energy was directed into political rivalries, exploitation of various scandals, and fear of anarchist attempts at assassination (bombs had even been thrown into the Chambre des Députés). The middle class had established itself at the expense of the lower and poorer classes, hence the shots fired at Foumiers and the strikes at Carmaux. But the bourgeoisie was so safely ensconced that its possible overthrow was at no point considered a real threat. It was ready to make the most of the *Belle Epoque* without a backward glance. And for the moment it was charmed by everything Russian: the novels, the squadron in Toulon, the Tsar and Tsarina who visited France.

Paris had recently been greatly altered. The new Eiffel Tower had risen dizzily against the sky since the universal exhibition of 1889, and almost all the writers and artists were scathingly critical of the 'odious pillar of riveted iron'. But in New York the first skyscraper was already standing. At Montmartre the new Neo–Byzantine basilica gleamed with its white towers. Just next to it the architect Baudot was about to build Saint–Jean–l'Evangéliste using concrete, a technique still limited to a few experts. The tenement houses in solid hewn stone had no style at all.

The first flying machines were about to lurch into the air. The biograph was a curiosity. Roentgen had discovered X–rays. The

2
CARRIAGE
1900

3
Two Women
in Town Clothes
c. 1904

first cars sowed panic in the countryside. The bicycle with its pneumatic tyres gained many enthusiasts. Horse carriages still dominated the streets.

No doubt these streets were already noisy, at least in Paris, but one could still wander along them, and enjoy the lively posters painted by Willette and Chéret. The crowd still dressed with full formality. A dark frock coat, worn with top hat, bowler or boater, cane and gloves was the order of the day for a man. Beards, moustaches and whiskers were worn as long and bushy as possible.

Colour was the prerogative of the army: the red and blue uniforms, edged with white, were set off by the officers' gold stripes, by plumes, feathers, and braid; all this gave an operatic air to the army demonstrations, which were much enjoyed by the crowd.

The women wore dresses down to the ground, high collars, layers of frothy lace petticoat, pitiless corsets laced up under camisoles, long gloves, muffs, little veils, hats covered in ribbons, feathers, flowers, fruit and birds. Even all this was not always considered enough to protect them from stray glances: fans and parasols filled in the gaps.

Furnishing was the preserve of the mistress of the house, and fashion dictated a great accumulation of objects. Often imitated from the past, furniture served less to furnish, it seemed, than to fill up as much space as possible. Sofas, benches, little fireside chairs, stools, folding screens and fire-screens set up as many obstacles to movement as they did to sight. Curios, plants, 'art bronzes' weighed down the shelves. Draughts were considered extremely dangerous. To prevent them, there was no limit to the number of cushions, curtains, and draught-excluders. Once night fell further protection was built up against the outside world; the paraffin-lamps were lit, and within the circle of their light, the family gathered peacefully together to read or sew.

To go on a journey it was necessary to have an important reason and special clothes to withstand the dust and smoke. Trains were yellow, green or deep red; they already travelled at some speed, but comfort was slight. From the popular spas, or seaside resorts (Deauville was dethroning Trouville), people sent their friends picture postcards—another recent invention.

The Côte d'Azur was an unspoilt paradise where a few invalids went in search of winter sun, but where none but the insane would dream of risking their lives in summer.

In Paris a passion for the theatre dominated all else. Mounet-Sully, Sarah Bernhardt, Réjane and the younger Coquelin reigned over the stage; the *avant-garde* was represented by Paul Fort, Antoine and Lugné-Poé. The Folies-Bergère, where Loïe Fuller danced in her long floating veils, was very popular, as were the circus and the new Moulin Rouge. It was the great era of the can-can, black stockings in a sea of petticoats—the world so brilliantly depicted by Toulouse-Lautrec, that of the cabarets of Butte Montmartre, the *café-concerts,* the happy carnivals with tons of many-coloured confetti.

And if people enjoyed themselves so freely and unashamedly it was no doubt because serious matters were treated seriously. Manners, education, the family, money and the state were never questioned. Young girls did not walk down the street alone. They

4 Georges–Antoine Rochegrosse THE DEATH OF BABYLON 1891

played the piano and did needle–work. 'Respectable' women did not work. Visits were frequently exchanged. The strictest mourning placed entire families in black for years.

Bourget, Loti, Anatole France, and Emile Zola, whose naturalistic descriptions made people shiver, because they found them *risqué,* were being read. Science was still reassuring, for the moment.

Art was also reassuring. What was accepted and admired, the work which competed for prizes in this bourgeois traditional society, had to be a mirror free of mystery, an image which would not arouse any uneasiness. This world found its own likeness in the popular illustrated papers: *La Vie Parisienne, La Fin du Siècle, Le Courrier français.* Caricatures were produced in plenty, but their method of attack was remarkably monotonous: it consisted in systematic distortion, and in putting huge heads on to minuscule bodies. Once the formula was accepted, it was scrupulously followed.

The accepted painters were those that showed in the Salon (with a capital S because it was the gallery where the rewards and medals were distributed), that is to say the artists of the official school. They alone had the right to be considered by the authorities and the public, and were under a much more stringent yoke than the outsiders *(Ill. 4).*

Realism was the law; the most short-sighted, petty and commonplace realism in the history of art. It had learned nothing from the noble classicism of David, the sensual precision of Ingres, or the robust appetite of Courbet; nor would it learn from the familiar poetry of the minor Dutch masters, redeemed by their pleasant subjects and the charm of their light. This dreary and academic naturalism was concerned only with exactness of drawing and with literal and faithful rendering of colour. It was a style of accuracy carried to the point of illusion. It came into competition with photography, then at the very height of its static period; family albums contained rows of studied portraits, neatly frozen into their poses. Photographically reproduced, the portraits painted by the professionals are hard to distinguish from original photographs.

The naked women who predominated in painting had all the immodesty of suggestive photographs: more undressed than nude, doubtless they were compensation for a fashion which allowed only an ankle to show. Any excuse was good enough; models in the studio, a bride getting up, also nymphs, sirens or witches at a sabbath.

Historical painting flourished, but it mostly dealt with insignificant subjects, cluttered with figures in costumes and accessories; the effect was one of laborious reconstruction. Genre pictures were the most popular of all. News items, social gossip, satirical songs, these were the subjects of the anecdotal style. Popular sentimentality fed on enamoured cuirassiers, little pastry cooks, choirboys and cats nestling in baskets. The official painters who were so much in demand were, in decreasing order of celebrity: Bonnat, Meissonier, Carolus-Duran, Henner, Rochegrosse, Roybet, Delaunay, Jules Breton, Morot, Ferrier, Chocarne-Moreau. The list can be limited to these.

To follow in their footsteps their successors needed only application and some manual skill. All they had to do was to obey the teaching of the Ecole des Beaux-Arts, which worshipped the past, believed in a unique and unalterable perfection, and taught only the tricks of the trade. The cult of precise drawing, exact colour and

5 WHITE FEATHERS 1919

6
Édouard Manet
PORTRAIT OF
IRMA BRUNNER
c. 1882

superficially true reproduction resulted in a mediocrity and uniformity unparalleled in the history of art.

To the great majority of people living at that time, this was the only sort of art, fulfilling their exact expectations, a natural and logical consequence of the great classic art forms that they also so admired. The sort of art which, for us, has taken over this historical role was born in opposition to its era, at first unnoticed, but later exposed to scorn, sarcasm and even anger.

It was born against its time, nurtured by a few clear-sighted artists who were only too aware of the errors of established artists and felt their own private obligation to make changes. From the day when Manet *(Ill. 6)* took on the responsibility of a vital break with the established order, in his *Luncheon on the Grass* at the Salon des Refusés in 1863, these artists accepted solitude as well as freedom in their painting, committed as they were to an adventure with no guarantee of success. As Matisse was to say, it was Manet who 'first made the immediate translation of his feelings, thus freeing the instincts.'

Complete abandonment to all sensations became, soon after, the hallmark of the impressionists. In fact, even more than the *impression*, rather a vague and subjective concept, the *sensation* remained their constant preoccupation, a sensation as pure and sincere as possible in its translation into paint. In this they show themselves to be utterly scrupulous realists, contrary to the belief that their works were eccentric scribbles. In fact Monet, Renoir, Pissarro and Sisley created their own tones, not by using their intellect but by working out an exact reproduction from relationships determined by light Witnessing an ever-changing natural scene, they managed to put into their pictures the reflection of the slightest gradation of the weather or season, and even the time of day, like optical mechanisms with extraordinarily sensitive powers of recording. Their painting, formulated at some distance from theories, remains the expression of a simple and sensual happiness, that of rediscovered innocence in the heart of a weary civilization.

By the early 1890s the movement had passed beyond its phase of unanimity. Its dealer, Durand-Ruel, who supported it steadily during the difficult years, organized large exhibitions of paintings by Monet, Renoir and Pissarro, thereby establishing their reputation. Monet painted his various series: *Haystacks, Poplars,* and *Rouen*

Cathedral, which had considerable success, before elaborating the lyrical chromatism of the *Water Lilies.* Other dealers, Petit, Boussod and Valadon began to take an interest in the impressionists, and at last, after thirty years indifference, collectors were beginning to add them to their collections. This was still not really a public success; the audience had simply become a rather larger one. For the average contemporary, for the Academy, for the public authorities, and for the curators of museums, the impressionists remained ignorant and nefarious daubers, unworthy of attention, and not to be introduced into respectable society. Meanwhile, impressionism, by its vigorous determination, gave birth, while it lasted, to other movements, and to strong personalities who used its discoveries to elaborate different modes of expression and to open up, in their turn, new horizons.

The neo-impressionists, or divisionists, under the impulse of Seurat and then Signac, attempted by the juxtaposition of dots of pure tone (simultaneous contrast) to reconstitute on the spectator's retina the equivalent of a natural luminous sensation while simultaneously seeking harmony of composition, measure and rhythm. Cézanne *(Ill. 10)* who was concerned with the quest for the

8 DINNER TABLE 1897

permanent behind appearances, the secret geometry of forms beyond their exterior attraction, produced some carefully pondered works, with the aid of a multitude of planes, saturated by colour, which determined shapes and volumes in space. 'There is a logic of colour,' he stated, 'the painter must obey only this, never the logic of the brain.'

This was a major victory, a victory for the autonomy of the canvas and the priority of its own demands over that of the subject. The 'distortions' that so shocked everyone, were only distortions when compared with the ordinary utilitarian vision of the world. In reality they are demanded by the logic of the medium. But towards 1890 such a triumph was still half-clandestine. Cézanne held aloof from Paris. Some of the people who had once known him even wondered whether he was alive or dead. When in 1895, Ambroise Vollard showed a collection of a hundred and fifty of Cézanne's canvases, they were a revelation to many young painters, who were immediately enthusiastic.

The brief and tragic adventure of Van Gogh, ended by the pistol shot of July 1890, was also unknown to the majority of people, and the news of it did not go beyond his small circle of intimate friends. Vincent had given himself up to colour as to an addictive drug; he had already foreseen in his 'Dutch period' that 'colour in itself expresses something'. The cult of Delacroix, the example of Japanese art which had recently arrived in Europe, and his trips to Paris, had rapidly helped him to emancipate himself from the first objects of his admiration: 'What Pissarro says is true, the effects that colours produce by their harmony or disharmony should be strongly exaggerated.' After his arrival in Arles, during a frenzied bout of work, he did indeed force himself to 'exaggerate the essential', to 'strengthen all the colours', and soon he was able to remark: 'Instead of trying to reproduce exactly what I see in front of my eyes, I now use

9 LANDSCAPE, TOULOUSE 1900

10 Paul Cézanne STILL-LIFE *c.* 1890

colour more arbitrarily in order to express myself more strongly.'
His colour did not long retain its impressionist iridescence, nor was
it carefully organized in modulations of space as it was with Cézanne;
since it was not bound to appear true to life, but to suggest senti-
ments, the 'terrible human passions', it carried the tonalities of
objects to their extreme by neglecting their transitions.

Van Gogh's burning self-revelation was only later to have world-
wide repercussions. Yet, the year after his death the Salon des
Indépendants organized a first retrospective showing of ten canvases,
and in 1892 sixteen of his other paintings could be seen gathered in a
small exhibition organized by Le Barc de Boutteville, a dealer who
had set himself up in the Rue Le Peletier in order to support contro-
versial artists.

Gauguin *(Ill. 13)*, for his part, wanted to reach 'the mysterious
centre of thought', rediscover the savage, the primitive, the 'fathom-
less enigma' of idols; to do this he pursued an energetic method
tending, in the manner of the great art forms of the past, towards

11 STILL-LIFE WITH A BLUE PATTERNED TABLECLOTH 1907

simplification and synthesis. With him painting once again became
flat, colour was spread over vast surfaces with generous brush
strokes, divided by sombre outlines which both isolated and emphasized them. Since colour is itself *enigmatic*, he thought that it was
permissible to use it in an arbitrary fashion, both with the harmony
of the picture in mind and so as to create a symbol. Its own vibration
led naturally to its expansion. 'I observed,' wrote Gauguin, 'that
the play of shadows and lighting in no way gave a coloured equivalent to light... What could be its equivalent? Pure colour!'
'It is,' he continued, 'our imagination which makes the picture
when we confront nature.'

   In this he was in agreement with the principles of the symbolist
movement, which had asserted itself in literature in 1886 in the
manifesto of the poet Jean Moréas, and which during the 1890s
was the focal point of *avant-garde* opposition to realism and naturalism.
The symbolists saw *ideas* as the supreme reality, so that the actual
form they took was merely their more or less sumptuous disguise.

12 NOTRE-DAME IN THE LATE AFTERNOON 1902

The ineffable, the irrational and the subjective were to be suggested, since by definition they could not be stated. Nature was only required to furnish equivalents, symbols allowing the spirit to escape everyday life in a flight of fantasy. At the same time poetry was seeking to avoid the banal, the direct expression, the 'too precise meaning'; instead it searched for the esoteric word, the rhythmic phrase, and *vers libre* was invented.

This effervescence of ideas filled both the important and the minor magazines. On the other hand never had the occult 'sciences' known such a success. 1889 may have seen the publication of Bergson's *L'Essai sur les données immédiates de la conscience*, but the occult work *Les Grands initiés* appeared at the same time by Schuré. The Sâr Péladan founded his mystical, spiritual, and artistic Rosicrucian Order. There was nothing, not even Catholicism, that did not feel the influence of this state of mind.

A certain school of painting found itself in agreement with this atmosphere; more perhaps that of Puvis de Chavannes than that of Odilon Redon, whose mysticism derived from 'docile submission to the arrival of the unconscious'. Redon himself was preceded in this path by a somewhat remarkable artist, the heir of Delacroix and Chassériau, but completely bound up with the imaginary: Gustave Moreau. 'I believe neither in what I see nor in what I touch,' explained Moreau, 'I believe only in what I feel. My brain and my reason appear to be ephemeral and of doubtful reality. Subjective emotion alone seems to me to be eternal and unquestionably certain.' One can see here an analogy with symbolist literature, indeed J.K. Huysmans, author of *Against Nature*, much admired Moreau's work, claiming to see in it 'magic visions, bloody apotheoses of other ages'. At first glance this art appears to be the epitome of literary painting in the worst sense of the word. His vast compositions are crowded with mythology, overburdened with colonnades, draperies and precious stones. However there was in them something other than mere decadence and *fin-de-siècle* pomp, something that much later André Breton and the surrealists were to pick up: a message in cipher emanating from the magic realms of the unconscious. In fact the structure of these paintings has nothing academic about it: the colours smoulder, the lines vibrate, and the great weight of detail itself attains a kind of grandeur.

Lastly, and however surprising it may seem, Gustave Moreau had the young Henri Matisse as his pupil towards the end of his career, and his influence over him was immense.

To complete this rapid summary of art between 1890 and 1895, mention must be made of the most advanced, and at the time, the most dynamic movement of all: a small group of men aged between twenty and thirty, united by strong ties of friendship and common convictions. Sérusier, Maurice Denis, Bonnard, Vuillard, Roussel and their companions, half in fun, half pompously, christened themselves the *Nabis* (in Hebrew: 'Prophets') having taken upon themselves the task of purifying and regenerating painting. First they looked to Gauguin, but also to Cézanne and Redon, and took a great interest in Japanese paintings and prints. The exhibition of Japanese art, organized in 1890 at the Ecole des Beaux–Arts, and the one mounted by Durand–Ruel in 1893, much impressed the young artists. In them they admired the simplifying virtues of the Japanese masters, and the results that they achieved with simple lines and blots. Following this example they attached great value to composition, often asymmetrical and unbalanced, they cut out shapes

14
PINK NUDE
1909

in silhouettes, juggled around with backgrounds to the very limits of legibility, and cultivated various shades of black. Their preoccupations were intellectual or spiritual according to the symbolist atmosphere of the moment. Moral, even apostolic, pretentions were not lacking, as the solemn letters exchanged by the members of the group show; they contain exhortations like these: 'Let us be pure in our spirits ! Let us be pure in our bodies ! So that our works can purify these sullied men, these miserable men, our brothers, and bring happiness to the poor, the abandoned, suffering under the yoke of others.'

Such a tone may seem naive. It is the result of the generous idealism of noble and disinterested young men who realized that by placing themselves on the fringe of the bourgeois order and the official world, they were condemning themselves to hardship and obscurity. At that time, any young artist who scorned the tracks laid down by the Beaux-Arts was committing himself to the unknown. While the masters of an independent style were still unaccepted, while Cézanne lived unknown in Aix, while the death of Van Gogh only merited two lines in a local newspaper, and Gauguin had to exile himself on the other side of the ocean, no early success was conceivable.

Artists were far less numerous then than they are now, picture dealing at that time had very little in common with picture dealing today. There were only three Salons in Paris. The official Salon, once the only one, split into two rival organizations in 1890: the Société des artistes français, and the Société nationale des Beaux-Arts. Both were strongholds of tradition, even if they did permit the occasional very mild audacity. Founded in 1884, the Salon des Indépendants incorporated every element that was alive and inventive, but of course this did not include the *avant-garde* alone. In Brussels the Salon des XX was an active and vigilant outpost.

Far from being counted in hundreds as they are today, galleries worthy of the name did not exceed a dozen. Very few of these accepted *avant-garde* art. Durand-Ruel, in the Boulevard de la Madeleine, was reaping the first fruits of the confidence he had placed in the impressionists during twenty years of effort and sacrifice. Georges Petit, Boussod and Valadon shared some of his success. In 1894 Père Tanguy died, the modest paint-merchant whose shop in the Rue Clauzel was frequented by the chosen few who came to contemplate the works of Cézanne and Van Gogh. The previous year a curious character named Ambroise Vollard, from the West Indies, who hid a very keen sense of the new values behind an assumed air of drowsy nonchalance, set himself up in the Rue Laffitte, a street of picture dealers. In 1891 the Galerie Le Barc de Boutteville organized the first exhibition of the Nabis, who were shown together on several occasions during the following years.

No quick money was made by these enterprising men; their cardinal virtues remained courage and a sense of adventure. Collectors who bought unrecognized styles of painting were rare, since their resources were generally limited, and it did not occur to them to speculate. Publicity was non-existent, and there were no prizes. The public museums of art were interested only in the past. Apart from the work of the official painters and the better-known impressionists, painting quite simply did not sell.

Vue de Ma fenêtre (Collioure)
HM.

2 Life and Work

The young man of twenty-three who, on an October day in 1892, got off the Saint-Quentin train at the Gare du Nord, had come to Paris to do his apprenticeship in painting, armed with his father's solemn warning, 'you will die of hunger' and a monthly allowance of a hundred gold francs. The decision he had just made was all the more difficult for coming so late. He had not been one of those infant prodigies who from a very early age show their irrepressible gifts by scribbling on the walls with charcoal or covering the margins of their exercise books with caricatures. Born on the last day of 1869 in Le Cateau-Cambrésis, a small town near Cambrai in the north, son of a seed merchant, Henri Matisse had been steered unprotesting into a legal career, more compatible with his delicate health than his father's trade, even though he had shown a certain facility in drawing-classes at Saint-Quentin high school.

He had therefore been sent earlier to Paris to prepare for his law examinations. A docile student, he had manifested no suspect curiosity in the capital. He had not even been tempted to visit the museums, or the annual Salon of Painting. He had occupied his free time with very ordinary diversions.

Once he had obtained his diploma, he had returned to Saint-Quentin, where he had been placed as a clerk in a solicitor's office. A life of honest and mediocre toil seemed to stretch ahead of him. If it was suddenly to deviate from this path this was due to chance. In hospital as a result of appendicitis he had followed the example of a patient in a neighbouring bed and passed the time by copying some colour prints with a box of paints he had received as a present. The unskilful reproduction of stereotyped landscapes, river banks and mills had unleashed in him, together with a sudden demanding enthusiasm, a need to know more. There were certain possibilities on the spot, the Ecole Quentin-Latour, for instance. The young clerk rose early each morning to attend some drawing lessons given by an old pupil of Bonnat's, between seven and eight in the morning, before going to the office. When he got home in the evening, he would study some manual on teaching oneself to paint.

It was at this point that the world around him was suddenly transfigured. He had become aware of beauty. The area around Cambrai is not without interesting monuments: renaissance, classical and baroque. Saint-Quentin possesses a Latour museum: its collection, if modest, has taste. The flat surrounding countryside was poor in subjects for a sketch; but a few familiar objects, a pile of dogeared books, a candlestick with its candle, arranged on a tablecloth, lit by the whiteness of an open newspaper, supplied matter enough for a scrupulous rendering of reality. This was the subject of Matisse's first known canvas, dated 1890, which he always kept *(Ill. 16)*. It is done in an astonishingly confident way for a beginner, and in the treatment of the floral designs on the tablecloth can be detected an approach curiously similar to that of Cézanne, which was all the more remarkable since the young man had never even heard of his name.

The conflict between his declared vocation and the tedium of his daily work had now begun; how could he continue to engross documents? From one month to the next such an existence became

16
STILL-LIFE
WITH BOOKS
1890

17 Gustave Moreau's Studio 1895

harder, the call to Paris stronger, and a break more probable. Once
he had actually accomplished this move, the artist was old enough
to realize its extreme seriousness. Sixty years later he was to remember with precision: 'Despite the certainty that I was on the right
path, and the feeling that I was in my element and no longer con-
fronted with a limited horizon, as I had been all my life... I took
fright, realizing that I could not turn back. I therefore hurled myself
into my work heeding the maxim that I had heard all my childhood:
"hurry".'

And he did hurry, to make up for lost time; he did what was
fashionable and necessary to start his painting career. He registered
himself for evening classes at the Ecole des Arts décoratifs and then
at the Académie Julian. At the former he had the good fortune to
meet Albert Marquet, who became a faithful friend, but at the

18
Gustave Moreau
AUTUMN
c. 1906

19
SLEEPING NUDE
c. 1906

Académie Julian he just missed Vuillard, Bonnard and Maurice Denis, who had left in the wake of Sérusier in order to found the Nabi movement, taking with them the influence of Gauguin. The professors revealed nothing to him, and neither indeed did the illustrious Bouguereau, hero of fashionable academicism, to whose antechamber a letter of introduction had taken him. The function of the Académie Julian was to prepare students for the competition for admission to the Ecole des Beaux-Arts. Young Matisse entered: he was turned down.

This was hardly an encouraging start. He could now attempt to work alone, or he could go to the glassed-in courtyard of the Ecole des Beaux-Arts and copy the antique plaster-casts. This is what he did. It was there that he had a providential meeting with Gustave Moreau, who interested himself in the young man's work, saw in it some good qualities, and agreed to take him into his studio *(Ill. 17)*, obtaining for him an exceptional exemption from the entrance examination.

The apparent contradiction between Moreau's public work and his influence on artists like Rouault, Matisse and Marquet, who all developed in such different directions from this common root, has long been a source of wonder. This relationship, and the attachment always avowed by his pupils, amounting in the case of Rouault to a sort of veneration, is explained by an exceptional intellectual influence, plus a particular talent for bringing out qualities, and an unrivalled generosity, discretion and intuition. He was a master in the best sense of the word. 'I am,' he used to say to the young people who listened to him, 'the bridge over which some of you will pass.' But for a bridge to span an empty gap effectively, the solidity of its arches must be tested. Today it seems probable that Gustave Moreau's pupils, frequent visitors to his house, at least suspected the existence of his vast quasi-clandestine output of sketches, in oils and watercolours, and preparatory drawings. Many of these are now gathered together in the Musée de la Rue La Rochefoucauld; their resources and virtues, heralding much later innovations, only began to be evaluated sixty years after the artist's death.

Rouault cannot have been the only pupil to be impressed by the powerful vividness of Moreau's blues and pure reds on a base of greens and dark violets, by the profound appeal of his chromatic

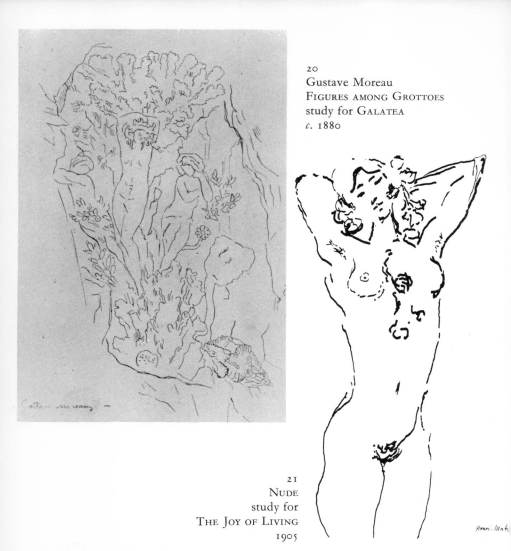

20
Gustave Moreau
FIGURES AMONG GROTTOES
study for GALATEA
c. 1880

21
NUDE
study for
THE JOY OF LIVING
1905

Henri - Matisse

alchemy. It was of this that the master was clearly thinking when he said in a lecture: 'If you have no imagination, you will never produce beautiful colours... Colours must be thought, dreamed, imagined.'

But most of all it is now no longer possible to ignore the direct influence of Gustave Moreau's styles of drawing on Matisse. For if one compares, for example, Moreau's *Autumn (Ill. 18)* with Matisse's *Sleeping Nude (Ill. 19)*, both dating from about 1906, the same slightly heavy insistence is found in both, the same thick stressed strokes, lined with violent blacks, and brilliant pale reflec–

tions, kept as if in reserve, the same way of enlivening the background by means of cross-hatching and dots, and even the same subtle treatment of the female body.

This relationship appears even more striking if one considers Moreau's drawing of *Figures among Grottoes (Ill. 20)*, a preparation for a composition entitled *Galatea*. This is in quite a different style, with simple, sharp lines, sinuous while at the same time imperceptibly broken at every turn. It is impossible not to recognize its influence in the many drawings in which Matisse traces women and plants using the same triumphant, elegant, and yet ceaselessly curved line, which of itself creates space, gives life to empty areas and distributes light *(Ill. 22)*. Not an elementary arabesque, but an essential one. As Gustave Moreau said: 'Art died on the day on which, in composition, a combination of reason and good sense took the place, for the artist, of the almost purely plastic imaginative concept: the love of the arabesque.' Almost half a century later Matisse was still echoing these words: 'It is the most synthetic way

22 NUDE STUDY 1936

of expressing oneself on all levels... The arabesque organizes itself like music, and it has its own particular tone... It conveys a collection of things with a sign and makes many phases into one.'

Also from certain sketches drawn by Gustave Moreau (for the *Triumph of Alexander* for example) came Matisse's liking for entirely filling narrow corners with ornaments, embroideries and flowers, and contrasting them with vast virgin surfaces; the combination lends great strength to the decoration.

Even in Moreau's rare sculpture one can find, strangely enough, some promise of what Matisse was to accomplish in this field. There are only a dozen wax figurines, which, he noted, 'cast in bronze, would give the measure of my qualities and skill in the rhythm and arabesque of lines better than in my painting.' In contrast to academic sculpture there is a sort of projection of drawing in space, of contours worked out in volume. Yet there is no evidence that these attempts, carefully preserved by the master in a cupboard in his rooms, could have come to the eyes of his pupils.

For the three years that he passed in Gustave Moreau's studio, where his strong personality was already making some impression on his fellow students, Matisse disciplined himself severely, allowing no exercise to be neglected and determined to learn his trade with the conscientiousness and humility that it required. The solid academic foundation that he set about building up for himself was based particularly on contact with the ancient masters, constantly recommended by his teacher. He did some twenty copies in the Louvre, mostly of Chardin and Poussin, but also of Dutch painters and of Raphael's *Baldassare Castiglione (Ill. 23)* and Annibale Carracci's *Hunt*. Several of these copies were bought from him by the state at very respectable prices. The choice of such models reveals in the young artist a wish to study, from the very best sources, the art of values, that is to say the degrees of intensity of light independently of colour, and muted and silvery harmonies. His own personal studies of that time were also treated in the same manner, views of the workshop of the Beaux-Arts. On two summer visits to Brittany, he also did some sea- and landscapes which caused his friend Evenepoel to speak of him from then on as a 'delicate painter, skilled in the handling of greys'.

However it was during this holiday at Belle-Ile that a disciple of

23
Copy by Matisse of
BALDASSARE CASTIGLIONE
by Raphael
c. 1894

Monet's first revealed to him the impressionist theories of the division of tone, vibration of touch and colouring of shadows. Under this influence he began to lighten his palette, to give shades to his greys and dark blues, and to use fresher greens. In his turn he discovered and began to collect the Japanese paintings on crêpe paper, which, despite the poverty of the means employed, had seduced so many of the Nabis by their expressive colours. To crystallize his recent experiences he decided to undertake a major work, a development of the numerous fairly conventional still-lifes that he had painted under the influence of Manet, in which he multiplied the contrasts and reflections with the help of glass and silver objects or fruit laid out on white tablecloths. In *Dinner Table* of 1897 *(Ill. 8)* one finds all these tricks occupying more than half of the canvas. But the change from the firmer style lies in the generous use of colours, which was divided, made iridescent, and enriched by delicate juxtapositions and punctuated by whites placed by degrees in order to underline the light coming from behind. More than to the impressionists, the work is related to certain Vuillards or Bonnards.

This new seduction of colour, quickened perhaps by seeing the

Turners in London, which Matisse visited briefly after his marriage at the beginning of 1898, led the artist to stay in Corsica, where he discovered for the first time the Mediterranean light which was later to dominate his work in such a vital way. Like so many other northerners, Matisse was overpowered by the sun-drenched splendour of the south, but unlike Van Gogh, who was oppressed by the sun beating on the burning roads, he came to tame and filter it, to use half-closed shutters on cool interiors. The history of the development of his art is that of the mastering of this splendour.

In Corsica, among the olive groves, in front of such luxuriant scenery, he retraced for himself the footsteps of the impressionists, adopting however a richer and better-blended touch and harmonies that were more alive *(Ill. 24)*. On his return to France, first in the region of Toulouse, then in Paris or on the outskirts, where he worked in the company of his friend Marquet, he persevered in this spirited style, highlighting it with shades of ultramarine, emerald green, rich and contrasting reds and oranges. They offer a very clear preview of future triumphs. Later Marquet was to describe their use of colour: 'We worked, Matisse and I... from about 1898,

24
CORSICAN
LANDSCAPE
1898

25 Pont Saint-Michel 1900

in what was later called the fauvist manner. The first "Indépendants" where I believe we were the only two painters to express ourselves in pure tones was in 1901.'

In 1898, however, though they had already attained this point of emancipation, Matisse and Marquet were still nominally pupils at the Beaux-Arts. But their master Gustave Moreau died that year, and his successor Cormon set out to impose the strictest academic discipline on the studio; the two friends left it for an academy in the Rue de Rennes where Carrière occasionally came to correct students' works, and where a new group consisting of Derain, Jean Puy, Chabaud, Laprade and others came under the influence of Matisse's strong personality. At that time he was an imposing figure, just turned thirty, quite tall, with a well cared-for moustache and beard. He might have been taken for a don rather than an artist.

Vlaminck described him: 'Blue eyes behind gold-rimmed glasses, reddish beard, Henri Matisse gave an impression of seriousness and had a vague air of a Herr Professor.' His friends nicknamed him 'The Doctor'; but they had a profound respect for his skill, his intelligence and the solidity of his convictions.

From this moment, he kept his distance from scholastic teaching and turned towards the true masters which he had chosen for himself: Van Gogh, and above all, Cézanne. His long study of the canvases of the latter warned him to be cautious in his turn of facile application of paint and superficial beauty of colours. In order to absorb the example better, he bought from Vollard, a great sacrifice for one in his financial situation, a small canvas of Cézanne's *Bathers,* which he was to cherish until 1936, when he made a gift of it to the Musée de la Ville de Paris. Under this influence he applied himself

26
NUDE STUDY
IN BLUE
1900

27
CARMELINA
1903

to constructing his still-lifes with minute precision without however ignoring perspective. From the window of his room on the Quai Saint-Michel, he tirelessly repeated the two magnificent views that he discovered: to the left the bridge with the head of the Seine lined with the trees of the Quai des Orfèvres, and restricted at the end by the roofs of the Louvre *(Ill. 25)*, to the right by Notre-Dame and the Ile de la Cité *(Ill. 12)*. In the many studies of these two views, he vigorously accentuated the different planes, insisting on the verticals and the long obliques, and often using the edge of the

43

28
LUCIEN GUITRY
IN THE ROLE OF CYRANO
c. 1903

window and the shutter to emphasize the strength of the foreground. As for the façade of the cathedral, it was often reduced to a monumental and synthesized H. Not long before at the Académie Carrière he had treated the male and female nude in the same way, simplifying the shape by means of energetic circles, translating the outlines of muscles by cobalt blue, and again using dark violet for backgrounds, while the luminous projections were conveyed by pure vermilions *(Ills. 26–7)*. These sombrely phosphorescent figures already show much more than a potential greatness. At the same time Matisse began his first attempts at sculpture. Interpreting Barye in the light of Rodin *(Ill. 158)* he worked incessantly at *The Slave (Ill. 157)*, for several years and hundreds of sessions, in a search for the means of condensing volumes without loss of expression.

The artist's second contact with the Mediterranean was to cause a sudden change of direction. When he arrived in Saint–Tropez for the summer of 1904, to join Signac and Cross in this still–unknown

village where it was possible to live well in the heart of beautiful
and unspoilt nature, Matisse found himself in a veritable stronghold
of neo-impressionism. Partly from curiosity, partly from a desire
not to miss a new experience, he adopted the doctrine of the movement, and forced himself to put into practice the principles of strict
division of tone, dotted lines, contrasts and shading off of colours
(Ill. 29). To start with, this was difficult and the results were
occasionally disastrous. But on his return to Paris, determined as
always, he applied the techniques of divisionism very strictly in a
vast composition of a beach surrounded by hills, a tall pine tree
parallel to the right edge of the painting, and a group of naked
women bathers gathered around a cloth spread out for a picnic.
Small rectangular and intermittent dots punctuate the sea, the shore,
the tree-trunk, the bodies and the clouds, decorating the whole
scene with all the shades of the rainbow. This canvas, exhibited at
the Salon des Indépendants in 1905 under the Baudelairean title of
Luxury, Calm and Delight (Ill. 32), gave rise to many different

29 VIEW OF SAINT-TROPEZ 1904

opinions. Today one might think that its fame largely exceeds its importance; the painter is clearly ill at ease in a borrowed style. A small sketch of the same subject shows a much more spontaneous feeling and an infinitely more alive series of colours. Both compositions lack naturalness, and the surface jerkiness is a most inappropriate rendering of 'calm' in the title; in addition the figures are badly integrated with the background, and the drawing itself, particularly of the reclining woman, is most unpleasant, the crowning disgrace for such an experienced draughtsman. It is not surprising, therefore, that after a few months he gave up this path, and spoke critically of divisionism as 'an often mechanical method which corresponds only to a physical emotion', adding: 'The breaking up of colour results in the breaking up of shape and contour. The result: a jerky surface. There is only one retinal sensation, but it destroys the tranquillity of the surface and the contours... Everything is dealt with in the same way.'

31 Page from L'ILLUSTRATION of 4 November 1905 showing fauve works in the Salon d'Automne of the year. Included are *Ills. 30* and *34*

Matisse did not abruptly turn his back on the method used by Signac and his friends. It would be fairer to say that he adapted it progressively to his own temperament, preserving only the advantages, eliminating the inconveniences, and gradually attaining quite a different conception. This transformation took place during the summer of 1905 at Collioure *(Ill. 15)* a small port in French Catalonia where Matisse once again returned to the Mediterranean of which he was so fond. But this was a different place from Saint-Tropez. The surroundings and the architecture of the town were more rugged, the light had the same brilliance, but was harsher. The landscapes that Matisse painted, alongside Derain who had come to join him, showed that the period of hesitation and borrowing was over. No more uniformly dotted surfaces; if certain areas remained speckled, they contrasted with other broadly modulated ones and served to put their calm strength into relief. His brush regained its complete autonomy; the canvas now delighted the eye by its unity. Extended until it became a thick and decided line, the brush stroke traced the shape, the intersections of buildings, branches of trees and contours of figures. Above all it retained the luminosity of neo-impressionism without losing its virtues through dispersal; instead its brilliance was concentrated in outlined surfaces, separated by 'silences' of bare white canvas. The strong colours—pure vermilions, pure cobalt blues, emerald green, all of course totally unrealistic—were united into a complete harmony only because they were joined to each other by milder but still unadulterated tones—pinks, mauves, yellows, pale greens and blues. The general effect was one of quite exceptional purity and well-being, as in *Open Window, Collioure (Ill. 34)*.

More than thirty-five years later Matisse recalled this turning-point in his work and confided to Pierre Courthion (in an unpublished conversation): 'During the time at Collioure I began with an idea that I had heard expressed by Vuillard, who used the word the "definitive touch"... This helped me a lot because I had the sensation of an object's colouring; I applied the colour, and this was the first colour on my canvas. I added to this a second colour, and then, if this second colour did not appear to agree with the first, instead of taking it off, I added a third, which reconciled them. I then had to continue in this way until I felt that I had established a completely

32 LUXURY, CALM AND DELIGHT 1904–5

harmonious canvas, and that I was emptied of the emotion that had made me begin it.'

The majority of the landscapes and portraits done at Collioure were shown with those by Derain, Vlaminck, Marquet, Manguin, Camoin, Puy, Valtat, Friesz and Rouault in Room 7 in the Salon d'Automne of 1905. (This Salon had first opened its doors two years earlier.) They unleashed a new scandal in the press and popular opinion, and earned the epithet 'Fauves' from the critic Vauxcelles. This word ('wild beasts') became the trade-mark of a movement. 'Fauvism', like impressionism and cubism, was a name bestowed by an outsider and not used by the artists among themselves. It has stuck, unlike the epithets of 'Invertebrates' or 'Incoherents' which were also used by hostile critics, because it is crisper and because its suggestion of beauty and strength is wholly appropriate.

To start with, fauvism was a gathering of a small number of artists completely opposed to affectation, delicate refinements, and the literary symbolism which was in favour with many of their contemporaries. Instead their temperament, and the example set by their great predecessors, led them to glorify in their own sensations.

Vlaminck and Derain, sometimes dignified by the solemn and imaginary title of 'school of Chatou' because they set up their easels in that still countrified suburb, looked towards Van Gogh and gave themselves up entirely to the violence of their instincts. But Matisse worshipped Cézanne, 'not for his pure, absolutely pure colours, but because Cézanne has been able to produce a powerful impact by the use of certain proportions, even with black and white'. And at a critical moment, when he renounced divisionism at Collioure, he found support in Gauguin for his conception of creative colour. 'But Gauguin cannot be placed among the fauves, because he had not found a way of constructing space by colour.'

The fauvists were thus all agreed to delegate full power to colour,

33
PASTORALE
1905

accelerating the evolution already begun some time before. 'The impressionists' paintings,' Matisse later told Raymond Escholier, 'have shown the following generation that colours, while they can serve to describe things or natural phenomena, have in themselves, independently of the objects they set out to express, an important action on a spectator's feelings. Thus simple colours can act on intimate feelings with all the more impact for being simple. A blue for example, accompanied by the radiation of its complementaries, acts on feelings like the sound of a gong. It is the same with yellow and red, and the artist has to be able to juggle with them when he thinks necessary.'

In another remark recorded by Georges Duthuit, Matisse gave his own personal definition of fauvism: 'The search for intensity in colour, the substance being unimportant. Reaction against the diffusion of local tone in the light; the light is not suppressed, but expressed in a harmony of intensely coloured surfaces.'

Such a conception of colour taken to its logical conclusion was, without doubt, a throw-back to certain works of the past: sparkling miniatures and cloisonné enamels of the Middle Ages, Slav icons, and, still further back, Byzantine art: there is nothing more fauvist, particularly when seen from near, than the mosaics at Ravenna or Constantinople. The technique of the juxtaposition of marble cubes or brightly coloured enamels, producing a necessarily simplified pattern, presents astonishing analogies with the style of the new painters of 1905. Later Matisse himself was to remark on these relationships, 'I understood Byzantine painting when I stood in front of the icons in Moscow'—this was in 1911; and much later still he was to have photographs of the mosaics of Hagia Sophia, Constantinople, in his house.

He used intense colour, often pure colour, but not, except very occasionally, applied straight out of the tube on to the canvas as has often been suggested. Fauvism cannot be reduced to so elementary a principle and Matisse again stated that the use of pure colours (begun by Gauguin and Van Gogh) was in no way enough to characterize the movement: 'This is only the outward sign. Fauvism came from the fact that we completely abandoned imitative colour, and that with pure colours we obtained stronger, more evident simultaneous reactions; equally important was the luminosity of the colours.'

This emancipation of colour from reality could be seen as an echo of Baudelaire's prophetic exclamation: 'I should like the meadows dyed in red, the rivers in golden yellow, and the trees painted blue; nature has no imagination.' The fact that these words are so unfair —nature gives every proof of a highly developed imagination in all degrees, from the infinitely large to the infinitely small—does not detract from man's legitimate demand for liberty of re-creation. In this sense fauvism constituted the first essential break with subjugation to the natural order of things, and paved the way for the total independence attained by abstract art.

The majority of the participants in the fauvist movement, which as such had only three or four years' existence, did not go beyond the stage of instinctive fauvism, a passionate glorification of the

35 LANDSCAPE, COLLIOURE study for THE JOY OF LIVING 1905

means, finally reducible to a variety of 'wild impressionism'. Dazzling as was the firework display given by Vlaminck or Derain, they nevertheless rapidly found themselves at the end of their resources, faced with the impossibility of striking still harder, of finding yet more incandescent pigments than the pure chromes and vermilions they already used; so they branched off, one in the direction of dramaticized Cézanne, the other towards a renewed classicism.

Matisse alone, for whom the fauvist period as such was only one stage among others, was able to go yet further, and draw even more possibilities, and still more powerful ones, from colour. The following ten years, from 1906 to 1916, marked a critical period, during which his researches were the most fruitful and the most profoundly original of his career. But, before examining them, it would be useful to catch up with his personal situation at the time when fauvism was established.

He was at last freed from immediate anxieties. The days of 1900, when necessity obliged Matisse and his faithful friend Marquet to join the commercial decoration teams of the Grand Palais, were already far behind. Since then there had been several modest sales mounted by Berthe Weill at her new gallery in the Rue Victor-Massé, where she zealously and disinterestedly supported the new painters. Vollard also, even though he was a more cautious figure, had put on, in 1904, Matisse's first one-man exhibition. Two years later, the Galerie Druet, in the Faubourg Saint-Honoré, organized a second exhibition with more material, and had a notable success.

Meanwhile, and most important of all, a small group of collectors had actively interested themselves in Matisse's work. The critical role played by these clear-sighted and courageous patrons must be underlined. Like all true lovers of art they were ahead, not only of contemporary taste, but also of the artistic discoveries immediately preceding them: while the impressionists, Gauguin and Cézanne were still being debated, these collectors were already looking ahead and perceiving the meaning of subsequent discoveries at the very moment when these were being decided. An extremely rare gift, and one of the highest merit, since it anticipated ratification by public opinion by thirty to forty years.

Matisse's first patrons, who made it possible for him to develop freely at a time when his work was to reach a crucial stage, were the Stein family, Americans living in Paris (the writer Gertrude Stein, her brothers Leo and Michael, and her sister-in-law Sarah), the French politician Marcel Sembat, a collector by inclination and a critic by conviction, and the Russian merchant Shchukin, owner of Cézannes, Renoirs and Gauguins, and until 1914 the buyer of many of Matisse's most important canvases. In their turn the Steins recruited other patrons from among their compatriots, such as Etta and Claribel Cone, while Morozov, another Russian collector, followed the example set by Shchukin.

The improvement in Matisse's financial situation allowed him to satisfy his taste for travel; he went to Algeria, northern Italy and Munich. Above all it enabled him to carry out some vast compositions without the need of immediate returns, to work on them for

36 THE JOY OF LIVING 1905-6

a long time or even, if necessary, to start them again. In one of the most famous, called *The Joy of Living (Ills. 35-6)* he takes up the subject of *Luxury, Calm and Delight*, but treats it in a completely different way. Once again there are figures in a landscape (sixteen instead of seven), expressing the joy of original life in the midst of nature and nostalgia for a lost Eden where work, constraints, clothes and sadness are excluded. The naked figures dream, dance, play the pipes, pick flowers, embrace, or simply revel in their own beauty and in that of the world. This time the colour, though still flamboyant, is spread out in vast flat tints, enlivened occasionally by highlights, such as the brushstrokes in the grass in the foreground. The rhythms are strongly marked, in the long sinuous lines used in the painting of the tree trunks and of the heavy foliage at the top of the picture, as well as in the contours of the bodies, emphasized by heavy strokes. For the first time, the actual drawing of the figures

37 Luxury 1907

38
LUXURY II
1907-8

deliberately fails to respect anatomical accuracy, in order to fit in better with the general organization of the picture; each figure reacts in relation to the others. This effect, however, is not obtained without some loss: some figures are mannered, others are heavy. Finally, several faces are suggested merely by a simple oval, without any

39
MARGUERITE
1906 or 1907

40
STILL-LIFE
WITH ASPHODELS
1907

41
LA COIFFURE
1907

indication of eyes, nose or mouth, an extreme abbreviation that Matisse was again to adopt towards the end of his career.

Several other compositions, in the following years, were to develop from *The Joy of Living,* treating and expanding some of his ideas. These were to give proof of a skill all the more impressive in its achievement of concentration in the elements of the work.

In *Luxury (Ill. 37)* three female figures, with one dominating the entire breadth of the canvas and receiving the homage and attentions of the other two, are integrated into a harmonious and detailed landscape of shore, sea and hills. The subject is treated in large sections of delicately-modulated colour. An essential change here is that violent colours have been abandoned for browns, earth colours

42 BATHERS WITH A TORTOISE 1908

and a dull green. The three bodies are painted in ochres, pinks and greenish tones. In a second version *(Ill. 38)* even all the iridescences have disappeared from the canvas and the tones are totally flat. The impression of happy plenitude comes, as the artist intended, from the generosity and exact proportions of the forms. He explained his drawings in the important *Notes d'un Peintre*, published by *La Grande Revue* in December 1908.

'What I pursue above all is expression... I do not think that it can be conveyed by passions fleeting across a face, or even by violent movements. It is to be found in my entire painting: the area occupied by figures, the empty spaces around them, the proportions, all these play their part. The art of composition consists in being able to arrange the different elements which the painter has at his disposal to express feelings in a decorative manner. In a picture, every section must be visible and play its own role, whether this is a principal or secondary one. Everything that has no function in a painting is therefore detrimental to it. A work of art entails a harmony of the whole; any superfluous detail would thus take the place of an essential detail in the mind of the spectator.'

A direct illustration of his words can be found in a contemporary work, commissioned by Shchukin to decorate a dining-room. It again takes up this problem, more directly that in *Luxury*, but once again in pure colour. A curious transformation even took place, because *Dinner Table (Ill. 48)*, first painted, and exhibited in the Salon d'Automne, in a harmony of blues, was then taken back and altered, and arrived a few months later at its buyer's house, changed into a harmony of reds. The mystery can be cleared up if one turns again to Matisse's article: 'If I spread shades of blue, green and red onto a white canvas, every time that I add a stroke, each of the ones I painted earlier loses its importance. For example, if I have an interior to paint: I find in front of me a cupboard, which gives me the sensation of a good bright red, so I put on a red that satisfies me. A relationship between the red and the white of the canvas is thus

43 BOWLERS 1908

established. If I add a green beside it, or render the idea of the floor
by yellow, there will again be relationships between this green or
yellow and the whole of the canvas which will satisfy me. But these
different tones will be mutually diminished. The measures that I use
must be balanced so that they do not destroy each other. To prevent
this I have to order my ideas, so that I find some relationship between
these tones which shows them off instead of destroying them. A
new combination of colours will succeed the first and provide the
totality of my representation. I am obliged to transpose, and it is
for this reason that my picture appears totally altered when, after
successive modifications, red has taken over the dominant note from
green.'

In *Dinner Table, Red Version (Ill. 48)* a sumptuous carmine, covering three quarters of the canvas, has been substituted for the blue. Only a thin line separates the table from the wall, and both are hung with a red and blue flowered material, the three planes of the table can be distinguished from that of the wall by the different directions of the flowers. The blue–black of the servant girl's bodice, the bright note of the fruit scattered among the decanters and the green of the landscape that can be seen through the window, form the contrasts necessary to the maximum intensity of the whole. To understand the strictly indispensable nature of each element, one should first cover and then uncover the small triangle of the house in the top left-hand corner, and thereby appreciate the role taken by this subdued reminder of the dominant carmine red.

Matisse was to go still further towards 'this condensing of sensations which makes the picture' thanks to two vast decorative

45
BATHER
1909

46
WOMAN IN GREEN
1909

47
ALGERIAN WOMAN
1909

48 DINNER TABLE, RED VERSION 1908

compositions *The Dance* and *Music (Ills. 51 and 53)*, commissioned by Shchukin for his private house in Moscow. To carry out his subjects the artist gave up the idea of illustration by eliminating decoration and accessories. As he said: 'We are moving towards serenity by simplifying ideas and figures. The whole is to be our only ideal... This entails learning and perhaps relearning the handling of lines, which constitutes a sort of writing. This conciseness of form corresponds to the use of colours, which are reduced to three: a good blue for the sky, the most beautiful of blues (since the surface is covered to saturation, that is to say the point where the blue, the idea of absolute blue is entirely apparent), the green of the hill and the vibrating vermilion of the bodies. With these three colours I obtained the luminous harmony that I wanted, and also the purity of tint. The particular proof of this was that the forms modified themselves according to the reactions of the neighbouring colours. Because expression has its source in the coloured surface perceived

49
GIRL WITH A BLACK CAT.
MARGUERITE MATISSE
1910

by spectator.' Though coloured to saturation point the surface is not uniform; it is alive, light and transparent, due to the incessant variation of intensity.

The Dance (Ill. 51) takes up the round dance featured in the background of *The Joy of Living (Ill. 36)*, reducing the number of figures from six to five, and keeping fairly closely to the attitudes of three of them. This time the movement unfolds in an ellipse, exactly contained in the narrow rectangle of the panel; by filling it entirely an indefinite continuation of the dance is suggested, quite plainly inspired by the farandole at the Moulin de la Galette, but larger, magnified until it reaches the proportions of an eternal manifestation of human joy, in a pure rhythm.

Its counterpart, *Music (Ill. 53)*, is as static and calm as *The Dance* is dynamically joyful. The three colours are exactly identical, but

the two musicians and the three singers, standing up or crouching, punctuate an essentially tranquil background with their immobile bodies. And the way in which they are distributed suggests a clef followed by four notes on an imaginary stave.

From 1906 to 1910, in the intervals between his large composi-

51 THE DANCE 1910

52 Sketch for THE DANCE 1909

53 MUSIC 1910

54 MUSIC (SECOND STAGE) 1910

tions, Matisse carried out an important number of less ambitious canvases, but in which he continued, in different styles, his efforts to interpret expression through both colour and form. These were often still-lifes, in which (an idea inherited from Cézanne) there are very close relationships between the objects and backgrounds consisting of materials with bold floral designs or bright blue and red carpets *(Ills. 11 and 40)*. He also painted some portraits, among them half-length portraits of his wife and daughter Marguerite *(Ill. 49)*, which are particularly enlivened by the heavy strokes which surround the strong tones.

It was also during this period that Matisse had his first experience of teaching. Giving in to the pleas of a few young disciples, he agreed in 1908 to advise a small group of them, first in his studio in the Rue de Sèvres, the old Couvent des Oiseaux, and later, under the pressure of the growing number of candidates, in another disused convent, the Sacré-Cœur in the Boulevard des Invalides.

Matisse showed the same broad-mindedness, the same complete lack of dogmatism towards his pupils, who were almost all Scandinavians, Germans, Americans or Russians, as his own erstwhile teacher Gustave Moreau. While allowing them to profit from his experiences, and instructing them in Cézanne's method as well as in the great styles of art, he sought only to strengthen their own personal feelings. Unfortunately most of his pupils were too submissive, as so often happens, and never got beyond the stage of superficially imitating his style. Matisse soon grew tired of the whole enterprise and began to grudge the time and energy that it demanded of him. Later he was to speak disapprovingly of teaching: 'How painful it is to see true artists give a part of their efforts to help those who cannot act on their own. All they manage to do is hand them props, which allow them to grope towards creating some useless work, while they too could be better filling their time.' The academy shut its doors in 1911.

The previous year Matisse, accompanied by Marquet, had made a journey to Munich, specially to visit an exhibition of masterpieces of Muslim art; this took on a significance to which a great deal of importance must be attached.

At the beginning of the century, many insulated compartments still existed among the great forms of universal art. The schools of

art often then called 'exotic'—Far Eastern, Pre-Columbian, Islamic, etc.—were certainly known, and even closely studied, but only by specialists. For general teaching purposes, as well as for the majority of the public, however curious people were about them, they were carefully separated from the western tradition of the Renaissance and Antiquity, to which it would have been unseemly to compare them. It was still a long way from the familiarity of the encyclopedic art book, the imaginary museum *à la* Malraux, which spans civilizations, continents and millennia. Only the occasional artist, emanci-

56 Zorah Standing 1912

57 Persian Miniature *c.* 1590

pated from the strictures of the Beaux–Arts, perceived the universal
worth of these forms of expression, and realized what valuable
lessons they presented. Matisse was one of the first. As early as
1903 he had been extremely interested in the exhibition of Muslim
art organized at the Pavillon de Marsan in Paris. In Muslim art he
found a purity, harmony, independence from appearances, refinement and idealization of colour which he immediately placed along–

59
YELLOW DRESS.
ZORAH
1912

60
THREE
STUDIES OF ZORAH
1912

61
LANDSCAPE SEEN
THROUGH A WINDOW,
TANGIER
1912

62
MOROCCAN WOMAN
1911–12

75

side the art he most admired. He stated this several times very
clearly, once to Pierre Courthion: 'I was influenced by Cézanne and
the Orientals', and another time to Gaston Diehl: 'Revelations have
always come to me from the east. In Munich I found new confirma-
tion of my researches. Persian miniatures, for example, showed me
all the possibilities of my sensations. This form of art, with all that
goes with it, suggests a larger space, a truly plastic space. This
helped me to go beyond the painting of intimacy.' In Munich
Matisse was so interested that he collected a large quantity of
photographs of the miniatures, carpets and metal objects. Even if,
for a long time, his admiration remained theoretical, with no direct

64
ZORAH
ON THE TERRACE
1912

application in his painting, we see today that he was able to render the drawing of some objects with filtered colour and the result does sometimes coincide exactly with the effects achieved by Oriental illuminators. Several works of 1911 are proof of this: *Painter's Family*, *Red Studio* (*Ill. 200*), and *Blue Window* (*Ill. 55*). Gaston Diehl wrote: 'Matisse has borrowed even the most minute details from Oriental aesthetics: the principle of continuous decoration, surfaces entirely filled and divided into vertical and horizontal registers, linear combinations or borders of little flowers and window roses (also used in his ceramics), a bias towards superimposed objects, and views from above; the composition of essentially ornamented

65
MADAME MATISSE
1913

66
WOMAN ON A STOOL
1913–14

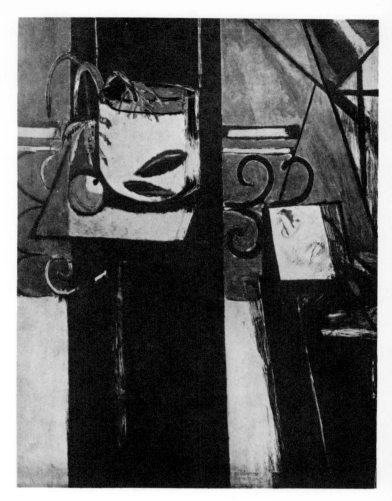

objects; a tendency towards geometrical exactness and occasionally
a border of intertwining vegetation.'

Matisse actually discovered the Orient a little later, at Tangier
(Ills. 58 and *61)*, where he made two winter visits in 1911 and 1912
(after his trips to the south of Spain and Moscow). Some of his
Moroccan models, men and women posing in local costumes for
group-paintings, naturally led him to return to the style of the very
large miniatures, evoked in an instant, for example *Zorah Standing
(Ills. 56–7)*; a flat silhouette, painted in green against reds; the huge
black eyes and the ornaments of the costume stand out vividly

against the extreme simplicity of the picture. But in these surroundings, where he was suddenly captivated by a window hung with
flowers, or in the luxuriant gardens or by the Casbah Gate, he
abandoned himself to the magic charms of superabundant nature,
which can be found in paintings such as *Goldfish (Ill. 69)*. The
colour is flower-like, enriched everywhere by delicate modulations,
deep and celestial blues, almond greens, pinks and carmines so
delicious that one would think they were scented. These pictures
are so permeated with happiness that they remain the witness of a
joyful moment, infinitely remote from care.

And yet care was never absent during those years, despite the
artist's successes both in France and abroad (his pictures had already
been shown in Berlin, Moscow and New York), and the way in
which his financial security had been assured by advantageous
contracts with the Galerie Bernheim–Jeune. His very successes,

68
Still–life
with Oranges
1912

69 Goldfish 1911

70
BOWL OF
GOLDFISH
1914

mainly abroad, gave rise to jealousy, envy and slander in certain
sections of the artistic world, and among art critics. At the same
time the rapid development of cubism (which gained some standing
at the Indépendants and the Salon d'Automne in 1911), and Picasso's
growing prestige increasingly captured the attention and approbation
of the young.

Cubism created a complete upheaval in painting, coming as it
did so soon after fauvism, and aiming at quite different results.
Appearances were shattered, forms dislocated; its austerity in
colours, which were often reduced to greys and browns, and the
introduction of a strange materials—cut paper, sand, wood, etc.—

were the mark of the dominance of the intellect over the sensations and of a search for realism carried as far as the use of actual objects; a piece of genuine newspaper stuck on to the canvas, instead of a representation or copy of the newspaper. Matisse, always so obsessed by all plastic problems, could not remain indifferent to these experiments, but he was too attached, both by training and by taste, to classical means of expression to allow himself similar liberties. Nonetheless, between 1912 and 1915, he painted a small number of canvases which appear to deviate sharply from his own style, and in which the influence of cubism, then in its so-called 'synthetic' period, is generally detected. No doubt it was never really assimilated into his work, but these sudden schematizations of form into clusters of straight lines, this triangulation of surfaces, seem deliberate and a little contrived; one can sense his uneasiness. These contradictions resolved themselves in 1916 in a series of large canvases, in which architectural preoccupations, introduced into Matisse's familiar world, resulted in pictures of admirable strength. One of the best examples of this is *Piano Lesson (Ill. 73)*, which is based on an interplay between tall verticals and incidental obliques marking out vast surfaces in flat colours, grey, blue, green, orange, pink, which describe the area of the room; the garden on to which it opens is merely suggested by a single green triangle. Against the wall, the picture of an enormously elongated woman sitting on a high stool blends with the shutters and curtains of the window, while at the same time the depth remains ambiguous. The direction of the light is daringly indicated by the dark triangle on the child's face, and the calm organization of the almost plain coloured surfaces is enlivened by the black arabesques of the window sill, as well as by the reversed letters of the name 'Pleyel' on the music-stand. This

72 Moroccans 1916

73 PIANO LESSON 1916–17

picture unites the abstract precision of a Mondrian with the quiet emotion of the best intimist paintings.

The same qualities can be found in the interiors of his studio on the Quai Saint-Michel *(Ills. 70–1)*, and in a series of still-lifes *(Ill. 67)*, in which the shapes are scattered around and stand out against abstract backgrounds, and where pure black makes its first appearance (foreshadowing the still-lifes of twenty-five years later, which

are very often treated in this way). They are also to be found in the
monumental composition of *Moroccans* painted in 1916 *(Ill. 72)* and
in the different figures which resulted from his Moroccan experiences.
In the former, Matisse transposes forms rather more than in most
of his works, so there is uncertainty whether some shapes are vegetable or human.

His development now took a new and decisive turn, governed by
a renewal of his longing for the Mediterranean. In 1909 Matisse had
settled down at Issy-les-Moulineaux, on the immediate outskirts
of Paris, on the edge of the Bois de Clamart, which had inspired
many of his tree and forest studies *(Ill. 74)*. At the end of 1917, he
arrived in Marseilles to join his friend Marquet, developed bron-
chitis and, in order to recuperate, went to Nice where the climate

had been recommended to him. The town, its setting, the splendour of the sea, the sky and the vegetation, so fascinated him that he was never to leave it again except for the occasional journey. 'When I realized that each morning I would wake to that light,' he later said, 'I couldn't believe in my luck !' He lived first in hotel rooms, settled next in the old part of the town, and then on the hill of Cimiez. Everywhere he went he repeated the motto: 'NICE: work and happiness', which he was to put at the bottom of a vivid poster painted for the town, during the last years of his life.

This happiness drawn from a privileged town, where blue and flowers were the decor of a natural and everyday feast, brought an immediate relaxation to Matisse's style, which gradually became gentle translation of the surrounding splendour. The output of the

76 Lorette in a Pink Armchair 1917

77
GREEN DRESS.
LORETTE WITH A
BLACK BACKGROUND
1916

78
LORETTE
1916

79
WHITE PLUMES
1919

80
WHITE PLUMES
1919

81
WHITE PLUMES
1919

82
WHITE PLUMES
1919

next seven or eight years has sometimes been labelled by the critics
as minor, but it is an art of pure delight and simple enjoyment of the
moment, set apart from his earlier major triumphs. Matisse was
clearly impelled towards more pleasant creations by leaving the
Paris crowds for his happy retreat in Nice, by the release of tension
after the war, and by his meetings with Renoir and Bonnard. Indeed,
he returned to the appearances of reality and in particular to the

laws of perspective, which he used with virtuosity, in views from above or below which were often combined with unexpected juxtapositions of subjects. Interior scenes became more common, with young women sitting or standing in front of windows *(Ill. 83)*, and, above all, there were dozens of odalisques, in different poses and disguises *(Ill. 87–8)* exploiting memories of Morocco. Bright colours were abandoned for nuances, water greens, pale blues, yellows and the lightest of greys.

In these paintings, even the smallest and most hurried ones, there is a marvellous certainty, exactness of proportion, variety

84
BLACK TABLE
1919

85 ARTIST AND HIS MODEL 1919

and elegance. This peaceable, balanced Matisse is no less true to himself than the Matisse of the great periods of conquest, and one does well to remember the warning formulated in 1908 in the *Notes d'un Peintre:* 'One often talks about the values of different methods, and their relationship to different temperaments. People like to draw a distinction between painters who work directly from nature, and those who work purely from imagination. I do not believe that one should preach one of these two methods to the exclusion of the other. For both can be employed one after the other by the same individual. He may need the presence of objects to receive sensations, and in this way even awaken his creative faculty, or his sensations may be already classified, and in both cases he can reach the same effect... The simplest methods are those which best allow the painter to express himself. If he is frightened of the banal, it will not be avoided by a strange exterior, by indulging in bizarre drawing or eccentric colour. His means are limited, almost by necessity, by his temperament. He has to have the sort of simplicity that will lead him to believe that he has painted only what he saw... People who continue to paint in a particular style and voluntarily disregard nature are estranged from truth. When an artist stands back to think, he must be aware that his painting is artificial, but when he is painting he must believe that he is copying nature. And even when he has moved away from this point, he must still have the conviction that it was done in order to render nature more completely.'

This period of Matisse's, the most accessible and sober, coincided with a marked reversal of opinion about him, a sudden concert of praise, as if the old fauve was a reformed character who could at last be admitted into polite society. The critics gave in. The official museum world took a first modest step by buying *Odalisque with Red Trousers (Ill. 107)* for the Luxembourg, and by conferring the Légion d'Honneur on the artist. On the international plane he was presented

86 ARTIST AMONG OLIVE TREES *c.* 1922

with the Carnegie Prize in 1927. All over the world there were exhibitions of his work, as well as monographs and books of reproductions.

However this success did nothing to make Matisse forget his own standards, or to influence his development, any more than his lack of success had before. He sensed for himself the danger of a facile manner and constant success. Between 1925 and 1929, a new period of reflection and trial took the place of his abundant production of *Interiors* and *Odalisques*. In his painting, colour was either applied more warmly in vast ornamental designs covering carpets and tapestries, or else much more sombrely. He made the most of the opportunities offered by drawing and engraving to investigate

problems in their simplest state. But it was his sculpture which showed most clearly his need for concentration and solidity. In several studies of heads *(Ills. 168–172)* the form was moulded with a freedom of style which makes one think of Picasso's most daring accomplishments in this field; the last stages of the great bas–relief *The Back (Ills. 177–180)* resulted in a monumental transposition bordering on abstraction.

Matisse was soon to find an occasion to satisfy the desire to do a colossal work, the vast mural decoration that every great painter sometimes dreams of. In 1930, having been invited to be on the Pittsburgh Jury awarding the Carnegie Prize that he himself had received three year earlier, he left for the United States. He first

allowed himself a three months' stay in Tahiti, where he was over-
whelmed by the charm of the South Seas; he drew and stored up
impressions that he was to use later. 'The light in the Pacific is
peculiar in that it has a sort of intoxicating quality for the mind,
like the sensation one receives when looking into a golden cup,'
was how he described it in an unpublished conversation with Pierre
Courthion. When he went to visit Dr Barnes, a magnate in the
pharmaceutical industry, and one of his most important collectors,
who also owned an impressive number of Cézannes, Renoirs and
Seurats, at Merion, Pa., the suggestion was made that he should
execute a large decoration in the building that Barnes had just had
put up to house his collection. It involved covering a considerable

89
YOUNG WOMAN
PAINTER
1923

surface, about fifty-two square metres. The problem was chiefly complicated by the way in which the surface was divided up, above tall french windows, and by the presence of three semicircular lunettes separated by the spandrels of the arches of the vault but joined together at the bottom by a long horizontal moulding *(Ills. 97–8)*.

Matisse decided once again to take up the theme of the dance that he had worked on twenty years earlier for Shchukin. But once in Nice, in the vast studio he rented specially for the work, his conception of it changed entirely. A less ambitious artist would no doubt have dealt with each of the surfaces separately, and contented himself with linking them together by some artificial means at the base. But from the start Matisse considered the three surfaces as a whole.

91 ODALISQUE 1923

92 ODALISQUE WITH MAGNOLIAS 1924

93 ODALISQUE WITH A GREEN SCARF 1926

94 ODALISQUE WITH AN ARMCHAIR 1928

He distributed his figures from one end to the other, and, playing with the possibilities posed by the problem, placed some of them at the critical points on the spandrels of the arches, in such a way that he managed to make one forget them, and so produced an effect of continuous motion. By cutting his figures at the edges of the composition, he furthermore led the spectator to prolong the movement beyond what could actually be seen, thereby suggesting a much larger composition. The final solution, which was preceded by many fruitless attempts, finally appeared when the artist, holding a charcoal pencil on the end of a long bamboo, drew a full-size outline at one

95
LARGE
GREY NUDE
1929

session. But when the drawing was finished, and it came to laying on the colour, new obstacles arose. Given the position against the light that the painting was to occupy, the colour clearly could not be weakened by nuances and modulations.

Matisse actually made the most of this back-lighting. 'I painted on to the panels,' he explained to Courthion, 'just above the piers, a deeper tone than on all the rest, a surface in pure black which is the darkest point of the picture. I thus created a tension between all the sections of the large wall, piers and panels. Thus when one saw the light from the windows, one also saw the blacks and the other colours.'

The tones were therefore reduced to four, spread evenly over the

97 THE DANCE (FIRST VERSION) 1931-2

98 THE DANCE (SECOND VERSION) 1932–3

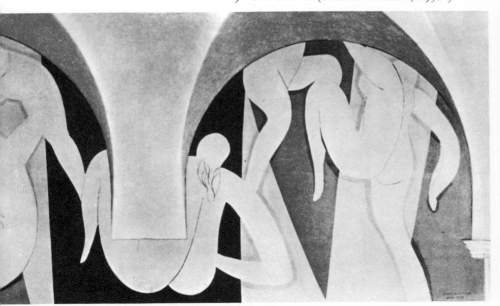

canvas: clear grey for the bodies, black, plain blue, and pink for the great bands of colour in the background.

In order to work with these elements and fit in with the architectural difficulties, the painter could only proceed by trial and error, ceaselessly modifying the partitioning of the colours. He did not allow himself the help of a reduced sketch, because as he had once explained: 'The composition has to aim for expression and modify itself according to the surface it has to cover... The artist who wants to transfer a composition from one canvas on to a larger one must, in order to preserve the expression, conceive it anew, modify it in its appearance, and not simply reproduce it on a larger scale.' Because of these circumstances, he introduced the use of coloured paper stuck to the wall.

After the composition had been finalized, and the paper cut-outs replaced by areas of paint (this, in itself, involved a number of last-minute changes), the time came to install the painting; but owing to an error in the original plan on which Matisse was working the spandrels were the wrong width.

A less exacting artist would have been able to adjust to the situ-

99
BLUE EYES
1935

100 PINK NUDE 1935

ation with a few partial modifications. But for Matisse the alteration of a single detail would have disrupted the whole picture. He took up work again and, in one new project after another, changed the entire composition, including the attitudes and positioning of the figures, which he increased from six to eight *(Ill. 98)*. The picture became even more animated, despite the fact that some of the figures were now seated, and the idea of wrestling vied with that of dancing. The emphasis on grace rather than elegance and the rhythm of the outlines demarcating the flat tints reminds one of the achievements of Greek art. Hellenistic in spirit, but stylistically independent, *The Dance* deserves a place in any of the most exalted buildings of our time.

After this interval, laborious and exciting at the same time, which lasted at least three years, Matisse rediscovered easel painting, and seemed to have benefited from his experiences; his work displayed a new freedom. The fertile period which now began, and which lasted twenty-five years, saw the uninterrupted flowering of an art ever more triumphant, without the hesitations or scruples of his younger years. From now on colour, carried to a supreme intensity,

101
HÉLÈNE
1937

102
MAUVE DRESS
1937

dominated; Matisse was also to make the most of expressive distortions. Details vanished, his abridged style introduced into painting the arabesque of drawing, inscribed as directly as with a pen. In the presence of such a blaze of colour some spoke of a neo–fauvism. 'When the means,' Matisse told Tériade in 1936, 'have been so fined down, so reduced, that their capacity of expression is worn out, one must return to the essential principles that formed the human language. These are the principles that revive and rejuvenate. Pictures that are refinements, subtle gradations and mellow colours without energy, cry out for strong blues, strong reds, strong yellows, subjects that stir the sensual side of man. This is fauvism's starting point: the courage to revive purity of means.'

In the interiors which almost always constitute the decor of these paintings, figures of women, their dresses becoming more and more sumptuous, tapestries, flowers, ornamental plants with jagged leaves are combined in an exuberant symphony. Straight lines yield to scrolls *(Ill. 104)*.

After 1933, Matisse gradually gave up sculpture, which no longer had the appeal for him that it had had at the beginning of his career. New techniques and preoccupations took its place. He exploited the memory of his travels in the South Seas in large-scale tapestry designs, at first fairly literal and then built up (as in *Polynesia*) with simple motifs of birds and marine fauna. He turned again to decors and costumes for the ballet. In 1920 he had designed Léonide Massine's *Le Rossignol,* to music by Stravinsky, for Diaghilev's Russian Ballet; in 1938 he undertook the decor and costumes for *L'Etrange Farandole (Ill. 109)* with music by Shostakovich, once again with Massine as choreographer for the Ballets Russes de Monte Carlo.

104
CONSERVATORY
1937

105 Music 1935

Most important of all, from 1930 he became interested in book illustration, conceived not as a more or less anecdotal accompaniment, but as a strong running parallel, a graphic equivalent of the text. The series was inaugurated by *Poésies* by Mallarmé (Skira, 1932, *Ill. 150*) with etchings in pure crystalline lines. This was followed by James Joyce's *Ulysses* (1935), Montherlant's *Pasiphaé* (Fabriani, 1944, *Ill. 151*), where the simple technique of linocut engraving produced dazzlingly white pictures against a perfect black background. In *Visages* by Pierre Reverdy (Editions du Chêne, 1946), and the *Lettres de la religieuse portugaise* (Tériade, 1946, *Ills. 152* and *153*), he tried out lithographs, treated with a size and precision hitherto

unknown. Lithography was again used for *Repli* by André Rouveyre
(Editions du Bélier, 1947), *Les Fleurs du Mal* by Baudelaire (La Bibliothèque française, 1947, *Ill. 154*), Ronsard's *Florilège des amours*
(Skira, 1948, *Ill. 155*) which was the most important because of its
size, 126 illustrations, *Poèmes* of Charles d'Orléans (Tériade, 1949,
Ill. 156) and finally Georges Duthuit's *Une fête en Cimmerie* (published
by Tériade only in 1963, though the 31 lithographs were done in
1949). The album entitled J*azz* (Verve, 1947, *Ill. 110*) is rather different: to accompany his lithographs coloured with paper cut-outs he
himself composed and wrote with his large and even hand a text in
which memories mix freely with confidences.

These techniques suited the artist all the better since illness had

106
READER
WITH A BLACK
BACKGROUND
1939

107 ODALISQUE WITH RED TROUSERS 1922

108 ODALISQUE WITH MAUVE AND WHITE STRIPED GOWN 1937

limited his physical activity. In 1941 an intestinal condition forced him to undergo a serious operation, and from that time he was obliged to spend the greater part of his day in bed, in some pain and suffering from insomnia. Matisse not only bore this trial with fortitude, he transcended it completely. His last work, benefiting from the domination of mind over body, reflects a marvellous youthfulness and a fertile vitality, a godlike synthesis of all he had learned during a long life. To artists and lovers of art he was a god, surrounded by universal admiration and respect. His face took on an expression of benign gravity. Dressed in soft, ample woollen garments, with his eyes bright and blue behind his glasses, his beard neatly trimmed, he appears in a film made in 1946 by François Campaux.

Whether at Cimiez, or in his house 'Le Rêve' at Vence, his household was scrupulously organized around him, like a three-dimensional Matisse. A desk enabled the master to work while lying down, a revolving bookcase stood within reach. A long, light bamboo pole with a charcoal pencil attached to it made it possible for him to draw at a distance (even on the ceiling). Lydia Delektorskaya, a fair-haired Russian girl, whose calm beauty inspired many sketches, was his secretary and assistant as well as his model.

For some time a large room was transformed into an aviary, full of hundreds of rare and exotic birds including pigeons and white doves which flew around freely. Large green plants, rubber plants and philodendrons brought the garden right into the house, standing on the furniture or in glass cabinets were *objets d'art* from all parts of the world: African masks, Polynesian statuettes, Japanese pottery, tapestries, and superbly written Chinese inscriptions. Still more numerous were Matisse's own works, his old sculptures and drawings, and increasingly large paper cut-outs, stuck on the wall to await their final form, or their transformation into ceramics or stained-glass windows.

In such an atmosphere, it might seem surprising that Matisse should give up four of his few remaining years of life to the great and risky enterprise of the Vence Chapel. 'A church !' said Picasso to Matisse with some irritation, 'Why not a market ? Then you could paint fruit and vegetables...' 'What's that to me ?' retorted the painter of *Aubergines,* 'I have greens that are greener than pears, and oranges more orange than pumpkins !—so why on earth should I ?' Until then, Matisse had not involved himself in any religious commissions. His serious illness in 1941 no doubt gave a new gravity to his meditations. He had been touched by the devotion of a Dominican nun who had nursed him back to health. In 1947, when living at Vence, his villa on the side of the mountain dominating this small, charming old town behind Nice, he was visited by another nun from the same order, who had once been his nurse in Nice. She mentioned to him a project for a chapel that the Dominican nuns hoped to build for their convalescent home nearby. Frère Rayssiguier, a Dominican novice, preoccupied by the problems of architecture in relation to the new liturgy, also approached Matisse about the same project, and the artist suddenly offered to take it on.

Matisse immediately perceived that within his reach lay the possibility of undertaking, not a monumental decoration like *The Dance* at Merion, but a work of which he would be entirely master and on which he could try out all his different plans. His idea was to 'take an enclosed area with very small proportions and give it, by the interplay of colours and lines alone, infinite dimensions'. The architecture itself, based on a design by Rayssiguier under the nominal supervision of Auguste Perret, made no pretentions towards originality. It was simple and followed a precise programme: an area for prayer for twenty nuns and eighty members of the laity; these demands required two perpendicular naves of unequal size, and the orientation of the altar at an oblique to each of them. Light came from the openings in the south and west walls, while the east and north walls were blind. Hence Matisse's second datum: 'to balance a surface of light and colour against a plain wall covered in black drawings on white.'

The chapel is completely white. White outside, like the surrounding houses scattered against the green where cypresses show up like black spots. Inside, the white walls, ceiling and tiles reflect the stained-glass windows: two groups of six and nine parallel bays, very narrow, but the entire height of the wall, and two large twin windows in the west wall.

From the beginning the subject and the general composition of the three large mural panels was fixed: the figures of *St Dominic,* the *Virgin and Child,* and the *Stations of the Cross,* in black lines on

white and executed in ceramics. The windows were to be in a
subdued colour range, prepared by the familiar procedure of coloured
cut–outs. But during the four years, one preliminary study succeeded
another, ceaselessly modified and ceaselessly simplified.

Each part was established through dozens of preparatory drawings,
very full and elaborate at first, later reduced little by little to their
essentials when placed in the perspective of the whole. Thus the
Virgin was entirely started over again seven times in her full size:
her mantle, scattered with stars and with large panels open to her
dress, finally disappeared to be replaced by a single contour, bare

09
DANCER
design for
L'ÉTRANGE
FARANDOLE
1938

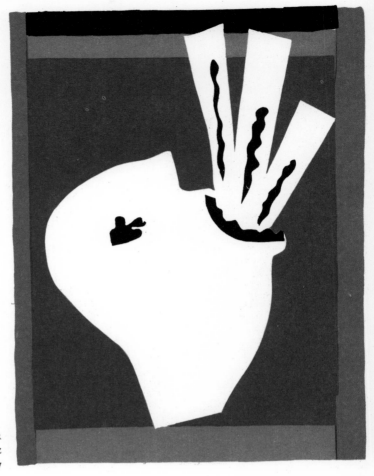

110 SWORD SWALLOWER
from JAZZ
1947

of ornament. The floral decoration that surrounded it, originally very involved, was sacrificed in favour of large, almost abstract flourishes *(Ill. 112)*.

The great figure of *St Dominic (Ill. 111)* was posed by Père Couturier, a friend of Matisse's and a Dominican, famous for his part in the reviving of religious art in France through an appeal to the best artists. Matisse did a twin figure of the same saint (black lines against a yellow ceramic) for Notre Dame d'Assy, in the Alps, the first church in which artists like Léger, Bonnard, Rouault, Lurçat and Bazaine collaborated in the decoration. Couturier's high and noble

111 WINDOW, ALTAR, and ST DOMINIC Notre-Dame du Rosaire, Vence, 1947–51

112 ALTAR, VIRGIN AND CHILD and part of the STATIONS OF THE CROSS
Notre–Dame du Rosaire, Vence, 1957–51

stature is clearly recognizable in *St Dominic,* even though the face
is reduced to a mere oval without eyes or lines. Matisse pointed out
to Couturier that: 'only Christ has a face in the Chapel—the one on
St Veronica's veil—to illustrate clearly that He alone must impose
His personality on us, while each of us has the right to imagine that
of the Saints.'

The *Stations of the Cross (Ills. 113* and *221)* was the most discussed
panel, and shocked several people by its extreme simplification.
The fourteen Stations, instead of traditionally lining a real 'path' are

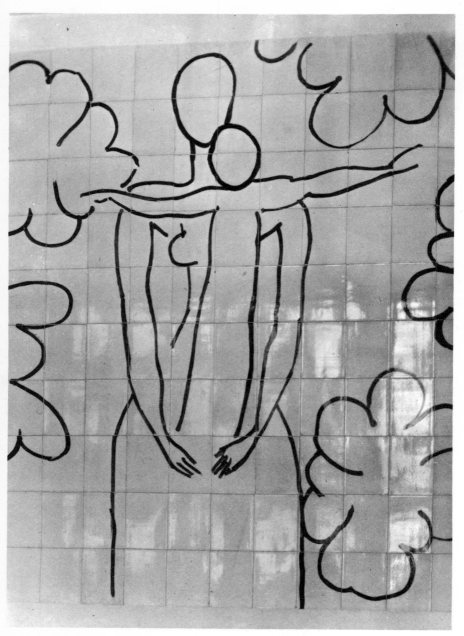

VIRGIN AND CHILD, detail of illustration 112

113 STATIONS OF THE CROSS Notre-Dame du Rosaire, Vence, 1947–51

gathered together on a single panel so that the eye follows a winding
road from the bottom to the top, guided by numbers. As they reach
their ultimate degree of concentration these scenes lose whatever
narrative and harmonious elements the sketches had still preserved, and express only the most violent emotions, as befitting the
Passion. 'What I see,' wrote Père Couturier, 'resembles a large page
covered in lines like the faded, hardly legible writing that one finds
in letters written in haste, under the shock of some very great
emotion, and in which one perceives already, without yet having
deciphered them, the clearest and most upsetting signs of what one
is about to be told.'

However, independently of the way in which the *Stations* themselves are arranged, the composition depends entirely on a large
pyramid of bending or kneeling figures. The hill of Calvary at the
top, on each side an oblique made by the two crosses and the ladder,

and everything converges on the body of the crucified Christ. The apparent chaos in fact conceals a very marked rhythm. 'Thus,' wrote Père Capellades, 'this barrenness, this continued poverty, this starkness which shocks at first sight, is necessary in order to attain the perfect and natural unity of the work as well as its true significance... One cannot therefore speak of baldness of style or schematization in this context. We see instead the plenitude of a style reached by the purity of line, infallibly guided by an artist who has attained the supreme height of his powers, and who is deeply living what he expresses.'

The stained-glass windows gave rise to detailed studies of colour and light; there were three stages of full size sketches *(Ills. 129–130)*. On a basis of very simple plant motifs, in broad proportions, Matisse created a harmony of fundamental colours—ultramarine blue, lemon yellow, and bottle green—whose delicacy is due not to the material (he wanted simple, very ordinary glass) but to the relationship between them. Indeed, this is so skilfully handled that these cold colours against the white inside wall produce an effect of rose-violet light of the rarest delicacy. 'One cannot introduce red into this Chapel,' Matisse said, 'nonetheless, red is here and exists by reaction in the mind of the spectator.'

The door of the confessional is an admirable tracery of carved wood, that reminds one of an Arab screen subtly playing on asymmetry using similar elements, circles and squares. On the altar, a sober and massive stone table, delicate chandeliers surround a crucifix which was also designed by Matisse. The scrolls of metal which hold up the sanctuary lamp are reminiscent of those of the lofty wrought-iron cross which supports the bell at its base, and rises like a miniature steeple more than twelve feet above the roof. The Madonna and Child figure once again on two ceramic medallions outside, and on the left of the entrance a small glass window unites the motif of the star with that of the fish caught up in the meshes of the net. Finally inside the confessional and in the sacristy are two painted crucifixes, white on black and black on white, less violent than those of the *Stations of the Cross*.

Matisse's work in the chapel also includes altar cloths, chasubles and copes *(Ill. 114)*. The chasubles in particular are remarkably effective. Also designed with the aid of paper cut-outs, they lend their vividness to the symbols of the liturgy—palms, fish, butterflies, ears of corn—accompanying the cross in sumptuous harmonies of violets, greens, lemon yellows, poppy reds, and a perhaps even more luminous black.

At the beginning of the summer of 1951, the chapel of Notre-Dame du Rosaire of the Dominican Nuns of Vence was blessed by the Bishop of Nice. Matisse, who was prevented from attending the ceremony by his doctors, sent a message in which he described this work as the culmination of his whole career. 'Despite all its imperfections I consider it my best piece of work. I hope that the future will justify this opinion by a growing interest.' His wish was that it be judged as 'the result of a lifetime devoted to the search for truth'.

Since then visitors from all over the world have flocked to Vence, and it has been generally accepted as the final synthesis of all his researches. But it must not be forgotten that the building was not designed for eager or merely curious tourists: it was destined to be a sanctuary precisely adapted to its role, a place of peace, solitude and silence, devoted to prayer and meditation. 'What I achieved in

114 VESTMENTS Notre-Dame du Rosaire, Vence, 1947–51

the chapel,' said Matisse, 'was the creation of a religious area', and 'again, I want those who enter to feel purified and freed from their burdens.' This aim was achieved by the use of all the available plastic resources to possess, as it were, the eye and the mind of all who entered. Matisse said in a conversation recorded by André Verdet: 'I built this chapel with the desire to lay bare my soul. I was offered the occasion to express myself in the totality of form and colour. This task was a lesson for me; I was able to set off rough materials against precious ones. They combined and shone by the law of contrasts. The multiplication of planes became a unity of plan.' It is precisely this unity of plan that lends the chapel at Vence its supreme quality.

However, it still remained for Matisse to add a codicil, by raising the technique of the paper cut-out to the rank of an art form in no way inferior to that of painting. In the extensive compositions that he carried out using this method, and in those he merely designed and which were later fixed in their final form by others following his instructions, he reached, with great boldness, a profusion of pure form in colour, as pure as can be imagined. 'There is no break,' he said, 'between my old pictures and my cut-outs; only with more absoluteness, more abstraction I have attained a form reduced to the essentials. All that I preserved of the object, which I once used to present in the complexity of its space, is the sign that is both sufficient and necessary to make it exist in its proper form and for the role for which it was destined.'

In 1950 the twenty-fifth Venice Biennale awarded him the major prize. Two years later the Musée Henri Matisse was inaugurated in Le Cateau-Cambrésis, his native town to which he presented another large and joyful stained-glass window for its infants school. On 3 November 1954 he died in Nice. His grave is in the cemetery at Cimiez; by providing his last resting place the town of Nice paid final homage to a man who, by his paintings, enabled the Mediterranean sun to brighten all the horizons of the world.

3 What is a Matisse?

There is no need for a detailed exploration of museums, or even of art books, to be able to differentiate with ease between a Flemish primitive and a work of art of the Italian Renaissance, or between a Dutch landscape of the eighteenth century and an impressionist painting. But you need a much finer 'eye' and longer practice to avoid confusing a Sienese master of the fifteenth century with a Florentine of the same period, or indeed a Monet with a Sisley of the same subject, both painted around 1875. An apprentice art-lover, before being able to identify a Matisse without hesitation among works by Vlaminck, Derain or Van Dongen, must master a first stage in which he will learn to recognize a fauve canvas, picking out what differentiates it from a canvas of the preceding generation, that of Van Gogh or Gauguin, to which, it is, after all, the direct heir.

Let us examine then, side by side, a supremely fauvist canvas, *Portrait with Green Streak (Ill. 117)* painted by Matisse in 1905, and *Schoolboy (Ill. 116)* by Van Gogh, dating from fifteen years earlier.

At first glance, these two pictures give out an equal impression of intensity. Both are close-up portraits, of striking immediacy without subtle colours; both are, right away, established in high colour registers, and Van Gogh's vermilion is in no way more powerful than Matisse's. In each case the backgrounds have no less value or importance than the portraits themselves (in contrast to the rules of classical portraits); *chiaroscuro* plays no part, and the strongest contrast is furnished by the dark blue mass of hair as opposed to the luminous colours of the rest of the surface.

However, one soon notices an essential difference: the contrasts furnished by the colours, which are more violent in Matisse's canvas, owe this enhanced strength to the fact that the tones are almost entirely unrealistic, while Van Gogh's, however heightened they may be, never conflict with natural colour, but are only a very extreme exaggeration of it. The boy's red hair is expressed by means of brushstrokes of different colours which together combine to give it its flame-like appearance. The greenish hues of his face are accentuated in the same manner as the scarlet of his cheeks, but there is nothing in this which has not been seen before, albeit to a lesser degree, in the work of Grünewald; similarly the pure red in the corner of his eye reflects anatomical truth in a way widely adopted by Rubens and many other 'traditional' painters.

This is no longer true of Madame Matisse's face as interpreted by her husband. The prussian blue used for her hair, eyebrows and eyes, the yellow ochre covering half of her face, the chalky pink on the other, and above all the famous middle pure green streak, which is also spread on the lips, chin and eye sockets, all bear no relation whatever to natural colouring. Let us remember the artist's maxim which stated that 'the dominant tendency of colour must be above all to lend itself to expression'. The forceful and, finally, even harmonious effect of Madame Matisse's portrait comes from the altogether arbitrary, but minutely calculated, use of colour.

The green line serves to express depth in a way that no other method could do as well: one only has to try covering it to see its necessity in the composition of the face, in relation to the three sections of the background, introduced with the whole canvas in mind (whereas the two backgrounds, red and orange, in Van Gogh's *Schoolboy* might very well indicate a wallpaper). The vermilion on the left-hand side of the canvas reinforces and enlivens the yellow half of the face, while the emerald shades on the right free the pink half from its artificial character. The result is that the face, which seen in isolation resembles only a carnival mask, draws its lifelike appearance and vivacity precisely from the different combination of colours.

The comparison of the drawing in the two canvases needs no less attention. Van Gogh's can readily be said to be, with no great abuse of language, realistic. A distinct line picks out eyelids, iris and pupils, models both the top and bottom lip, indicates teeth, outlines

116
Vincent van Gogh
SCHOOLBOY
1890

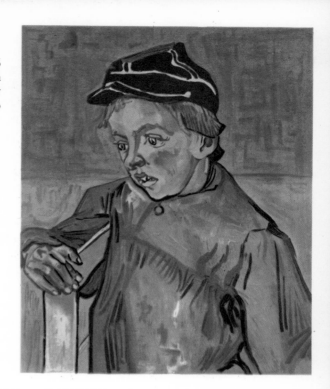

117
PORTRAIT WITH
GREEN STREAK
1905

the shell of the ear, and separates the different locks of hair. This concern for individual detail is impossible for Matisse by virtue of his choice of colour as a means of expression, a colour at once exalted and imaginary, which would never submit to the limits of a scrupulous drawing. The drawing is thus basically a result of the colour rather than the reverse: its lines are the natural frontiers of the colours, and so, by necessity, considerably simplified. In this way Madame Matisse's eye is rendered by an arc and a touch of colour in the same blue, her mouth by a single brushstroke in vermilion toned down by a repetition of the pale pink, her right ear is a simple suggestion in the red background, while the left is underlined by a thick bold line.

Such drawing, while it can be taken for a ruthless abbreviation, cannot yet be considered a distortion, given the vigour and conciseness of its lines. As far as a portrait of this kind employs them at all, the laws of perspective are in no way disputed; they are merely treated with benevolent indifference. (It should be enough to think of the tortures inflicted by Picasso on the human face to appreciate the relative restraint shown by Matisse.) Matisse could even completely blot out the features and reduce the head to a mere oval, without violating the basic structure of his models.

All this applies to Matisse's fauve period: a discussion of his later work is now necessary if the reader is to learn to identify all his many styles. At first glance, there is no obvious relationship between a *Portrait* of 1905, an *Odalisque* of 1925, and a *Figure* of 1940; in order to attempt an explanation of what they have in common, let us move on thirty-five years and examine one of the most famous canvases of the artist's last period: *Roumanian Blouse* of 1940 *(Ill. 123)*.

The first impression it makes is of a new and extraordinary simplification. Here is a painting in three colours, red, white and blue, very nearly without colour modulations, while the drawing is made directly onto the canvas with a paint-brush. This is 'two dimensional' painting, bare of any relief, with no concession at all to classical perspective.

A more detailed examination indicates that this simplicity is deceptive. No less than ten colours are in fact present: the three dominant ones, plus a pink, an orange, a carmine red different from that of the background, a yellow, a green on which rests the blue of the skirt and which appears against the joined hands, the deep grey of the hair, and a black, a larger number than in *Portrait with Green Streak (Ill. 117)* (which has eight: vermilion, purplish-blue, carmine, emerald green, green-yellow, ochre-yellow, pink, prussian blue and black). They are neither mixed nor applied uniformly, but are set off transparently against the white of the canvas. The composition is entirely made up of calculated asymmetries, the general inclination of the body towards the left being compensated for by the slant of the head and the swelling of the shoulder, which explains the bulk of the starched blouse and also the dominant role played by the top right-hand corner of the canvas.

The impression of opulence and luxury generated by *Roumanian Blouse* is largely the result of Matisse's treatment of the embroidery. These few whorls, these few points painted so negligently are the equivalent of the richest ornamentation imaginable, just as the few dots on the collar of the *Portrait with Green Streak* were enough to soften, by conjuring up an effect of lace, the severe violence of the whole.

The secret of such splendour conveyed by such economical means, which is one of the essential characteristics of a Matisse, is largely explained when one realizes that the final canvas was preceded by fifteen preliminary stages during which the painter, having once defined his subject, pruned it down to a final concentrated result. Sacrificing one thing after another—the model's skirt was initially decorated, and there were floral motifs in the background which have been first reduced and later done away with altogether, the sofa itself was abolished in the end—he was able, while cutting down on the embroideries of the blouse, to let them retain their full value and to make them the focal point of the picture, contrasting with the starkness of their context. Since we are unable to reproduce all the preparatory stages, five will have to suffice as illustrations of this method *(Ills. 118-122)*.

In his search for a plastic solution, Matisse, rather than proceeding with corrections and approximations, conceived the whole anew each time, and generally on a fresh canvas. 'At each stage I establish an equilibrium, a conclusion. At the next sitting, if I discover some weakness in the whole canvas, I use this flaw as a point of re-entry—

118–122
Five of the
Preliminary
Studies for
ROUMANIAN BLOUSE

123 ROUMANIAN BLOUSE 1940

and I conceive the whole all over again, in such a way that each part takes on a new vitality. Since each element represents but a fraction of the total strength (as in an orchestra), everything can be changed in appearance while the essential idea remains the same throughout. A black can very easily replace a blue, since basically the expression is derived only from the existing relationships. One is by no means slave to a blue, a green or a red. To make myself clearer: the picture will always be composed of blue, yellow and green and their proportions will be modified. Alternatively one can define the relations which make up a picture more exactly by substituting a black for a blue, just as in an orchestra a trumpet can be replaced by an oboe.

'In the final analysis the painter's emotion is totally spent and has been transferred entirely to his work. In any case he himself is liberated from it.'

'Harmony' and 'orchestration': here are two of the essential keys to discovering what features are constant in Matisse's work. A painting is born during successive stages, the total work being the sum of each level, but what seems to remain constant is this concern with an expression based on the quality, the exactitude of carefully determined relationships between the chromatic forces present in painting; neither chance nor theory plays any part, because it is completely dominated by an ulterior sensitivity.

We must now verify the preceding observations which are based on relatively simple works, by examining a structurally more complex canvas, for example *Still-life with a Red Carpet* (1906) of the Musée de Grenoble *(Ill. 124)*, considered by Matisse to be his best painting.

This is a very full canvas; the first impression is one of forceful assertion of the dominant red, but at the same time of an intense pullulation of colours and forms, a multitude of complex local relationships. Matisse's favourite theory, that subject and background are equal in importance, finds here a perfect illustration. The 'background' made up of carpet, tapestry and even wall, demands at least as much attention as the traditional elements of the still-life itself, fruit and objects.

Thus the problem, and it is a very difficult one, is to combine intense and ornate surfaces instead of simple expanses of colour; to orchestrate several groups of instruments, rather than isolated ones. The very orchestration of these groups is conducted with unsurpassable skill; the feeling of richness is not eventually derived from the diversity of the tints, but rendered instead by the multiplication of effects obtained from limited means.

René Huyghe, in an analysis of this category of effects, wrote with some perspicacity: 'If one places two colours side by side on a defined surface, the resulting pleasure is both keener and more durable, if, instead of juxtaposing the two tones in two neighbouring areas, one breaks up the whole of the surface into minute divisions in which the two tones cover the same total area, but alternating and blending together. A form of divisionism, no longer realistic, but "plastic"... for which Matisse sought a realistic pretext; everything that is active in nature was to fill his canvases from now on; striped materials, tapestries, oriental patterned pottery, juxtaposed flowers, and even alternating chinks in a closed shutter...

'Matisse's art consists essentially of giving the maximum gaiety to the pleasure procured from a colour, while retaining the maximum freedom.'

The painter often preserves this openness and freshness by the presence of quiet areas: neutral tones, black or white.

René Huyghe goes on to say: 'While it is more delicate, the problem remains the same for two coloured sensations. Each has to create a diversion from the other. In Young's accepted theory of vision, the eye perceives colour by means of three different neutral receptors, on which excitation produces respectively the sensations of violet, green and red (and not blue, yellow and red which Chevreul believed to be the only simple colours). One colour thus rests the eye from another by exciting a different nerve; hence the old theory of complementary colours.'

Here I must be allowed a brief digression. Matisse always insisted that his choice of colours was not based on any scientific theory, but that it was founded on observation, feelings, experience and sensitivity; and that, unlike Signac who was concerned with the study of complementaries, he sought only to introduce colours which gave an effect. But we know from experience that the instinct of a great artist— such as Delacroix—either precedes or reaches the same conclusion as any lesson derived from scientific observations.

However it is very strange how the theorists of the plastic arts, painters or critics, who, since the last century have devoted so much

124 STILL-LIFE WITH A RED CARPET 1906

attention to the laws of complementary colours, or more exactly simultaneous contrasts, have given so little thought to those, of an inverse but none the less striking effect, that physiologists and psychologists have derived from phenomena known as 'equalization'; and yet these were noticed in 1874, that is to say the exact date of the great impressionist flowering.

To give a very rough explanation, a surface of a given colour, once scattered with small patches of narrow lines of another colour, is attracted towards this other colour, instead of withstanding the contrast. A uniform grey crossed with narrow blue lines becomes bluish, or yellowish if these lines are yellow. This phenomenon can be observed by means of very simple experiments. Painters of all times have used this principle quite unconsciously with no scientific formulation, and in the case of Matisse, in particular, it would be possible to carry out a detailed analysis of the question, following his career from the beginning. The scope of this book forbids me to do this: however, *Still-life with a Red Carpet (Ill. 124)* alone furnishes several examples: the yellow floral designs on the wall tapestry visibly make the red more orange, while the blue and yellow dots of the tablecloth distort its red colour, making it either more purple, or a lighter red, and thus lending variation to this single colour which dominates the whole width of the canvas. And a similar effect can be detected in the dark blue and red visible on the green hangings.

It is now obvious that quality, exactitude and richness of harmony are the essence of a canvas by Matisse, and that these relationships do not depend on pre-established principles, but on the way in which they are put on the canvas. The artist himself suggested this extremely revealing comparison: 'A picture is made up of the co-ordination of controlled rhythms, and thus one can transform a surface which appears red, green, blue or black, into another which appears white, blue, red or green; it is still the same picture, the same sensation presented differently, but the rhythms have changed. The difference between the two canvases is that of the two aspects of a chess board during a game of chess. The appearance of the board alters continually during the game, but the intentions of the players moving forward their pieces, remain the same.'

The variety of colour harmonies introduced by Matisse was eventually very large. Nonetheless, it is possible to isolate a few of them which recur more often during certain periods.

Lemon yellow (whether used for fruit or not) against a black or dark background, or with bright reds and blues: *Dancer and Arm-chair, Black Background,* 1942 *(Ill. 140)*.

Bright vermilion under the favourite pretext of the goldfish, against very clear greens or blues : *Goldfish (Ills. 69* and *162)*; blue, red, pale greens: *Mauve Dress (Ill. 167)*; or blue, red, pink: *Young English Girl,* 1947 *(Ill. 226)* ; lastly black, a light, luminous black in relation to which reds, pinks, mauves and blues take on an exceptional vividness: *(Ills. 166, 223, 224)*.

To resume, let us group together the formal characteristics by means of which one can recognize a Matisse.

The role played by *colour* (intense or not) is of primary importance.

It is *unrealistic* ('When I paint a green, this does not necessarily mean grass; when I paint a blue, this does not mean sky').

It *indicates*, by relations alone, volume, space, light and expression. *Form* is simplified, but not 'stylized'.

Distortions are equally expressive, and depend on the demands made by colour. The *arabesque* is very frequently stressed, with a paint-brush or else dotted on with a new colour. Such a drawing often takes on, in the later years, an appearance of improvization similar to *graffiti*: checks, stripes, dots, which decorate certain parts of the canvas contrast with vast plain surfaces.

The *paint,* except in a few of his youthful works, is alway applied extremely lightly. It is completely bare of the *impasto,* superimpositions and corrections which so often crowd a canvas. Always becoming thinner and more fluid, during his last period it was often reduced to simple transparent scratches which preserved the trace of the rapid passages of the brush, while allowing an underlying stroke to remain visible. Quite often it did not even colour the whole canvas, but left white gaps exposed, which separated the areas of colour, and effected transitions between them.

Finally the sum and combination of these different means join together to create an atmosphere of luxury without ostentation, unassuming happiness, conciseness in the midst of abundance and, one might even say, a feeling of opulent simplicity.

It is to oil painting that one's first thoughts turn, without a doubt, when one thinks of a Matisse. But he produced many drawings, engravings, and sculptures which carry his mark no less strongly. Before examining each of these categories, we will begin with his paper cut-outs, which are in fact nothing other than a particular form of painting.

Paper cut-outs. The technique of paper cut-outs, originally a simple method used in the preparation of painted compositions (as for *The Dance* at Merion, and the decor and ballet costumes of *L'Etrange Farandole (Ill. 109),* and later for the covers of the expensive art review *Verve),* was gradually transformed between 1943 and 1947 into a technique of its own, used for producing finished works.

125 NEGRESS 1952-3

It is not the same as the cubists' use of *collage,* but retains some of its elements while adopting a different format and different aims. Picasso and Braque made use of existing materials (newspapers, cigarette packets, labels, bits of wallpaper) and scattered them around, completing the picture by charcoal or ink lines and areas of paint. The small compositions were based on the introduction of fragments of real objects into an imaginary space. Matisse used only plain coloured paper which he prepared himself by spreading gouache evenly, but not mechanically, on large sheets of white paper. In this way he obtained a matt surface, with no reflections, in the exact tone that he wanted. His range of tones was so bright in colour that his doctor advised him to wear dark glasses in his studio while he was not working.

He cut the forms he wanted directly out of these coloured sheets,

126
PARAKEET AND SIREN
1952

127
DECORATIVE COMPOSITION
1947

129–130
(Opposite)
Study for windows
for Notre–Dame
du Rosaire, Vence,
Second Stage
and Third Stage,
1950

128
CHRISTMAS NIGHT
Study for windows
in the Time–Life
Building,
New York,
1951

which were then pinned on to a white or coloured background and
he was thus able to study their relationships for as long as he liked,
simply by moving them around. This simple method made it
possible for him to draw directly in colour, instead of having first to
establish an outline. 'Cutting straight into the chosen colour reminds
me of the direct carving of the sculptor', he said. This procedure,
so apparently elementary and often used by young children, demands,
in fact, a very complex mastery of colours in their primitive, simple
state, and allows no possible nuances other than those created by the

balance set up between them. This lent his work an added youthfulness and strength and a previously unattained boldness.

Coloured studies of isolated motifs—rosettes, leaves, palms—
preceded more ambitious compositions, which gradually took on
gigantic proportions: *Negress (Ill. 125)*, *Sadness of the King (Ill. 135)*,
Parakeet and Siren (Ill. 126), *Pool, Acrobats, Large Decoration with
Masks*. Several of his pictures are based on the repetition of the
same element, which is modified by infinite variations of form,
absolute and yet never identical. As he said in *Jazz*: 'In a fig tree no

143

one leaf is exactly the same as another, but each one differs in shape,
and yet every leaf cries out: fig tree !' The richness of his work
comes from the infinite repetition of a particular element.

Let us examine *Sadness of the King (Ill. 135)* in the light of Matisse's
own remarks: 'An object must be studied at some length before one
can discover its symbol. And one must remember that once placed

132 TWO FRIENDS 1941

in a composition this object becomes a new symbol, which, while retaining its own strength, is nevertheless part of the whole... Thus the symbol out of which I create an image agrees with the other symbols that I have to determine as I go along and which are of course peculiar to this invention. The symbol is thus defined at the very moment at which I use it, and in terms of the object to which it belongs. This is why I cannot define my symbols beforehand; fixed symbols would merely resemble writing and would paralyse the freedom of my invention.'

Matisse went still further in the exploration of means of expression in the great gouache cut-outs of his last few years. It is due to these that he never sank back into the comfortable exploitation of past glory but remained, to the very end, part of the creative *avant-garde*. To be convinced of this one has only to consider his *Blue Nude* *(Ill. 133-134)*, one of several similar canvases. Taken as a whole, the superb elegance of form is in no way inferior to that of the female figures of the great periods of Matisse's painting. It is, however, very different. In isolation, no detail can be said to correspond to anatomical accuracy, and the articulation of each part is as remote from the truth as the rest. And yet the total truthfulness of this double figure is, in its entirety, very striking: a harmonious knot of limbs, each one elongated or distorted, with radically altered relative proportions. The human, vegetable and marine elements tend to exchange their qualities in a sort of single formulation. The blue paper in which the shape is cut gives one the impression of plunging into an elemental azure. André Verdet wrote: 'The intense blue of the paper is not there to symbolize the colour of the sea, but very simply because Henri Matisse, after lengthy experimentation, attributed to this blue a power of localizing, little by little, the origin of light and colour...

'The body is fixed in the present moment at the same time as it is freeing itself in the dynamism of the next moment. It is the wonder and exhilaration of outdoor life. By its very magnificence it stresses the primacy of the body, the movement of which diffuses plastic beauty and tends towards the ideal.'

Drawings. Matisse's drawings are executed in charcoal (or more rarely in pencil), pen and ink or with a brush and ink. These three very different techniques result in large differences in the work produced.

The drawings in pencil or charcoal, which often served as preparations for paintings, are very easily recognizable. They are not finished works, but rather mark a stage in the experimental development of a subject. This explains why the paper retains traces of the

133–134 Blue Nude III and Blue Nude IV 1952

preceding stages; the old lines, rubbed out but still visible, evoke the ghost of the shapes destroyed in favour of new ones, thus placing the final form in a sort of halo of memories. The lead or charcoal shading, rubbed with a smudger or a finger, has no connection with the light and shade playing on the real object, as it has in academic drawings. *Chiaroscuro* here defines a certain area in space, which the shapes may occupy in their successive movements. Next, the greys of the lead or charcoal provide an equivalent for colour and texture. Lastly, modulated in vast pools of harmonizing values, slightly obscured in some places, lit up in others, they create zones of sheen rather than light, quite independent of the light really playing on the model, and very delicately suggest a relief without carving it out or embossing it.

His pen drawings, done with broken strokes, are still more characteristic, and are better known. We saw earlier what they owe to

135
SADNESS OF THE KING
1952

136
NEGRO BOXER
1947

137 Snail 1953

Gustave Moreau. The appearance of ease is only superficial. If one of these drawings is examined very closely, preferably with a magnifying glass, it will be seen that the drawing is constantly inflected in its progress, and is made up of a multitude of infinitesimal sinuous lines, and even brief interruptions, which bring each point in the line to life. The genesis of this outline has been shown by François Campaux in his film about the artist, by using slow-motion photography. While the normal speed of the film shows Matisse in the process of drawing with certainty and speed, the same sequence in slow motion reveals a fragmented movement, ceaselessly correcting, as if every second he was choosing between several different solutions. Each of these choices leaves its mark in the microscopic inflections of the line. Matisse used to say that he unconsciously established relationships between the subject and the dimensions of his sheet of paper.

The appearance of this rough outline, the unconcerned speed with which the first connections are made, as seen in the line drawings, does not mean that these can be confused with what are normally called sketches. A sketch can be very laboured and elaborate, and still not go beyond immediate notation. These drawings are much more accomplished than the way in which they are done might at first lead one to believe. If they seem structurally simple, it is not because little of the subject was taken in, but on the contrary because much is eliminated, and that, as a result of a rigorous process of selection, what is retained is highly charged with meaning. What the line evokes, in fact, is not only the contour of objects and their position in space but also their values, ranging from light to dark.

139
LANDSCAPE
SEEN THROUGH
A WINDOW,
TANGIER
1912

140 Dancer and Armchair, Black Background 1942

The whiteness of the paper is in no way altered, but *qualified*. How? Matisse described the process himself, in his *Notes d'un peintre sur son dessin:* 'Despite the absence of interlaced lines, shades or half-tones, I still allow myself to juggle with values and modulations. I modulate with my line which becomes more or less heavy, and mainly with the surfaces that it delineates on the white paper, not by touching them but by approaching them.' Results of this sort do not usually come immediately, but appear as a reward for patient preparation. 'These drawings are always preceded by studies using a less demanding method than the pen, for example in charcoal or smudger, which enables me to consider, simultaneously, the character of the model, its human expression, the quality of the light surrounding it, its atmosphere, and everything else that can only be expressed in a drawing. And it is only when I have the feeling of being exhausted by this work, which can last several sessions, that, my mind clarified, I can let my brush go to work with confidence.' Drawings such as these will bear no corrections. Once completed they are either successful or not, and if not can only be started again from scratch, 'like an acrobatic feat', until the moment when the synthesis becomes total. At this point, not only are the values and the light enclosed in the white areas differently expressed, but also, to a certain extent, the colour which is re-established by the spectator's imagination in terms of the other particulars.

Finally, the role which falls to decoration is a very characteristic one and never pointless, but an 'answer to emptiness' as Valéry put it. The decoration—embroideries, necklaces, flowers or leaves, etc.—shows up and modifies the vast neighbouring areas which are left bare, by augmenting the density and complexity of black lines in certain parts of the paper. Matisse had every right to say: 'Jewellery or arabesques never overwhelm the model, because these jewels and arabesques are part of my orchestration. Carefully placed, they

141 WOMAN PLAYING A GUITAR 1939

142
NUDE STUDY
1936

143
SIESTA
1937

144
Beautiful Tahitian
1937

145
White Frill
1936

146 NUDE IN THE STUDIO 1935

suggest the form or accent of the values necessary for the composition of the drawing.'

A number of these drawings develop variations on the theme of a woman and a mirror *(Ill. 142),* which provided Matisse with an opportunity for two subjects, to trace the curves of the female body twice, rhyming the lines with each other. This is also a way of multiplying space. The model and its reflection alone are stressed, while the mirror is at times only suggested in its role of reflection. The artist's face is frequently included in the drawing *(Ill. 216),* or his hand is painted in the foreground *(Ill. 146),* as an indication of the importance of the actual act of drawing, the presence of the observer materializing what he sees; this acts as a signature even more definite than a written name at the bottom of the paper.

The brush drawings which were done by spreading an abundance of Indian ink over the paper and making cursory advances and bold splashes, date mainly from two particular periods in Matisse's career. The first is his fauve period. The use of a brush enabled the artist to paint quick sketches of a conciseness and rapidity unrivalled by any other method. This method was founded on his long experience of open–air sketching done with Marquet (who was also an expert at this) and by the example set by the Japanese. The other is the period between 1947 and 1951, when he used very thick brushes on large sheets of paper sometimes more than a metre high *(Ills. 148–9)*. Henceforth black was not only used for the fine network of lines, separating and determining the different kinds of whites, but competed with them as an equal, and attained an equivalent degree of luminosity. In many of the still–lifes, flowers, leaves and fruit are defined by large blobs of pure ink, at other times barely spotted,

147 STILL–LIFE WITH FRUIT AND A CUP OF COFFEE 1941

148
NUDE WITH
BLACK FERNS
1948

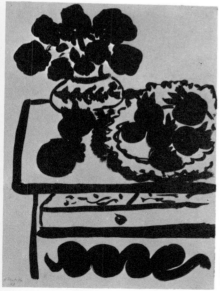

149
DAHLIAS AND
POMEGRANATES
1947

yet their colour is none the less evident. For the artist these drawings contained as many qualities as a picture or a mural-painting, because they attained a 'differentiation of the quality of surfaces in a unity of light'. This is why he used a thick brush when he prepared the interior decoration of Vence chapel, which was then carried out in ceramic mosaic.

Book Illustrations. Matisse's book illustrations never exactly correspond with the text; nor are they a literal commentary or paraphrase of it. 'The illustration must be the plastic equivalent of the poem.' But Matisse submitted himself with the greatest respect not only to the particular nature of the literary work, but also to the considerations of the techniques involved: typography, format, different sorts of engravings.

'I do not differentiate between the construction of a book and that of a picture, and I proceed always from the simple to the composite, ever ready to conceive of it again as simple. Working first with two elements, I then add a third, to the extent to which I believe it necessary in order to reconcile the two preceding ones by enriching the harmony—I might have said "musical-harmony".'

So for Mallarmé's *Poésies (Ill. 150)* Matisse decided to do etchings in order to reproduce their atmosphere of immaculate purity *(Sur le vide papier que sa blancheur défend...)* suggested by the key words: *glacier, lily, hoar-frosts, crystal, foam,* etc. But these were etchings in a regular line, very thin without shading, leaving the printed sheet almost as white as before printing.

'The drawing fills the page with no margin, which lightens it still further; the drawings in this case are no longer massed together in the centre, but spread out across the entire sheet... The problem therefore becomes one of balancing the two pages—the white one with the etchings and the relatively black one with the printed text.

'I obtained the desired result by modifying my curves in such a way that the spectator's attention is drawn as much by the white sheet as by the promise of the reading of the text.'

The extreme fineness of this cutting line is similar to that traced by a steel point on crystal; and is an admirable accompaniment to the adamantine poetry of *Brise marine* or *Hérodiade*.

The illustration from Montherlant's *Pasiphaé (Ill. 151)* gives the

150
Illustration from
Poésies
by Mallarmé
1932

impression of a negative of the preceding one: the lines are white against a background of absolute black, like a lino-cut. Matisse describes his method in *Comment j'ai fait mes livres*: 'The problem here is the same as for the Mallarmé, but the two elements are reversed. How to balance the black page of the illustration with the relatively white page of print? In the composition, by using arabesques in my drawing, but also by reconciling the engraved page with that of the text opposite in such a way as to form one unit. Thus the engraved part and the printed part strike the spectator at the same moment. My efforts were completed when I added a wide surrounding margin, across both pages, which completely joined them together.

'At this point in the composition I had a sudden thought that a totally black and white book would have a slightly sinister character. I know that a book is normally like this. But in this case the large, almost entirely black page seemed a little funereal. So I thought of using red capital letters.'

In fact, even without this coloured note, the black of the engraving is so illuminated by the brightness of the white lines—bold, frank, quite thick and drawn in a series of broken curves—that it is quite free of any sombre appearance. Matisse compared the gouge's work on the lino (the instrument which carves into the surface, the furrow corresponding to the white line) with the interplay between

151
Illustration from
PASIPHAÉ
nry de Montherlant
1944

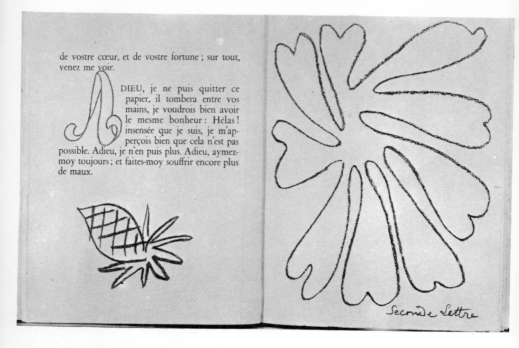

de vostre cœur, et de vostre fortune ; sur tout, venez me voir.

DIEU, je ne puis quitter ce papier, il tombera entre vos mains, je voudrois bien avoir le mesme bonheur : Hélas ! insensée que je suis, je m'apperçois bien que cela n'est pas possible. Adieu, je n'en puis plus. Adieu, aymez-moy toujours ; et faites-moy souffrir encore plus de maux.

Seconde Lettre

152
Two Pages from
Lettres de la
Religieuse
portugaise
1946

153
Marianna Alcoforado
study for Lettres
de la Religieuse
portugaise
1945

154
Illustration for
LES FLEURS DU MAL
by Baudelaire
1947

a violin and its bow: 'The gouge, like the bow, is directly connected to the sensitivity of the engraver. The slightest distraction during the tracing of the outline involuntarily results in a slight pressure of the fingers on the gouge which has an unfortunate influence on the line. Just as with a violin all you need to do is gently tighten your fingers round a bow for the sound to change from soft to loud.' Matisse speaks from experience; for a long time, like Ingres, he was a skilled amateur violinist.

In order to illustrate Ronsard, Charles d'Orléans, Baudelaire and the *Lettres de la Religieuse portugaise (Ills. 152–153)*, Matisse chose the technique of lithography, which allows line to retain its maximum subtlety and endows the chalk with a velvety softness; it is the ideal tool for conveying sensuality and emotion, and is as perfectly in tune with the love songs of poets as with the passionate cries of the putative nun Marianna Alcoforado. The choice of type proved at times to be difficult, particularly in the case of Ronsard *(Ill. 155)*. The text of Charles d'Orléans' *Poèmes (Ill. 156)* is not typographically printed, but handwritten by the artist; its illustrations are executed in different coloured crayons. Those of the *Lettres portu-gaises (Ills. 152-3)* are in brown and violet. This introduction of colour, even a single one as in *Florilège des amours (Ill. 155),* no doubt adds to the charm and attraction of the whole, but breaks the austere harmony of the black and white illustrations, which remain the most perfect compositions in the book.

The sculpture. Matisse's sculpture could not but suffer from the universal success of his painting. It has rarely been given the place it deserves, and remains almost unknown to many of the painter's admirers. Yet it is important, as much for its quality, as for its quantity (the exhibition in the Musée d'Albi in 1961, which, for the first time, accorded him the exalted rank he merits, gathered together no less than sixty-three pieces). During a great part of his career, the artist gave much of his attention and time to it. As he himself admitted, he devoted more than five hundred sessions, and several years of strenuous labour, to *The Slave (Ill. 157),* completed in

155 Two Pages from Florilège des Amours by Ronsard 1948

ÉLÉGIE A JANET
Peintre du Roy

Pein moy, Janet, pein moy je te supplie,
Sur ce tableau les beautez de m'amie
De la façon que je te les diray.
Comme importun je ne te suppliray
D'un art menteur quelque faveur luy faire.
Il suffit bien si tu la sçais portraire
Ainsi qu'elle est, sans vouloir desguiser
Son naturel pour la favoriser :
Car la faveur n'est bonne que pour celles
Qui se font peindre, et qui ne sont pas belles.

30

156 Frontispiece and Title-page from Poèmes de Charles d'Orléans 1950

1903. Before this he had already spent a considerable amount of time working on his first piece, openly inspired by Barye's *Jaguar Devouring a Hare*. *The Slave*, on the other hand, shows the influence of Rodin *(Ill. 158)* (then at the peak of his fame) in its pose, in the absence of arms, in the treatment of the strong muscles, and finally in its weathered appearance. Matisse had been introduced to Rodin, who, on seeing his drawings, advised him to use 'little niggling strokes'. But this was not what the young artist needed; he did not repeat the visit and rapidly changed direction in his style. 'I had already imagined on my own,' he said, 'a work of general architecture, replacing explicit details by a living and suggestive synthesis.' However effective were the 'pieces', they did not appeal to him, and in his eyes a juxtaposition of bits did not constitute a valid architectual design.

Later studies, contemporary with his fauve period, show the same

157
THE SLAVE
1902–3

158
Auguste Rodin
WALKING MAN
1877

concern for reducing form to its essential significance by subordinating detail to the whole and by exaggerating its prominent features. Several heads and female figures, culminating in *Reclining Nude* of 1907 *(Ill. 160)*, which is particularly characteristic of the period, show evidence of this concern. In this case the female nude is not a

159
MADELEINE I
1901

pretext for a virtuoso display of muscles, delicate skin, or quivering flesh—the effect sought by the sculptors of the eighteenth century, for example, and even by Rodin in *The Kiss*. On the contrary, expression is vigorously stressed in the way in which the pelvis flows and protrudes, in the contrasting angles created by the right arm leaning on the ground and the left elbow raised above the head, in the curve of the torso, the pronounced voluptuousness of the breasts and the splendour of the hair.

The fact that Matisse was exceptionally satisfied with this piece of sculpture has been more than proved by the way in which he used it as an important motif in several later canvases, in particular his *Sculpture and Goldfish (Ill. 162)*, and a canvas painted at the same time, *Blue Nude,* even adopts the exact position of the sculpture *(Ill. 161)*. Matisse bore witness to this correlation and the ties between the

sculpted and painted work in a significant description in a conversation with Courthion: 'I took up sculpture because what interested me in painting was a clarification of my ideas. I changed my method, and worked in clay in order to have a rest from painting where I had done absolutely all that I could do for the time being. That is to say that it was done for the purpose of organization, to put order into my feelings, and find a style to suit me. When I found it in sculpture, it helped me in my painting. It was always in view of a complete possession of my mind, a sort of hierarchy of all my sensations, that I kept working in the hope of finding an ultimate method.'

The female figure known as *Serpentine* 1909 *(Ill. 164)* almost belongs more to the vegetable kingdom, with its elongated and flexible body. The distortion of the torso and the legs gives a somewhat archaic look to the piece, which is completely different from classical sculpture. The thighs are extremely slender, while the ankles are as thick as one would expect the thighs to be; in fact this construction is repeated in one of the figures in *The Dance,* of 1910 *(Ill. 51)*. In this context African sculpture, the Etruscans, and art

161
BLUE NUDE
(SOUVENIR DE BISKRA)
1907

162
SCULPTURE
AND GOLDFISH
1911

163
Two Negresses
1908

of the Aegean has been mentioned, and we do know that Matisse
was one of the first people to take an interest in African statuettes
brought home by travellers at the beginning of the century as exotic
curios. For all this *Serpentine* cannot be related to African art, but
one can point to a much more striking similarity in the Gallo–
Roman statuette, also cast in bronze, discovered at Neuvy-en–
Sullias in the Loiret *(Ill. 165)*. A curious similarity is suggested by
the proportions, contractions and elongations and by its overall
rhythm. It goes without saying, of course, that I am referring only
to a slight similarity, but it is a sufficiently eloquent one to suggest
a reflection on the permanence of certain archetypal expressions
born on the same soil, and on the unexpected convergence of the
refinement of a contemporary master with the spontaneous feeling
of an unknown Celtic craftsman long considered a barbarian.

The creative evolution of Matisse's sculpture can be appreciated
very clearly by considering the valuable series of five busts produced

164
SERPENTINE
1909

165
NUDE WOMAN
Gallo-Roman

between 1910 and 1911, on the theme of *Jeannette*; they resemble five successive stages marking the transition from relative realism to bold transposition. *Jeannette I (Ill. 168)*, though carried out vigorously, maintains the regular features of the model's face, under a mass of drawn–back hair. *Jeannette II (Ill. 169)* concentrates these features by introducing the first elements of asymmetry: the hair line on the

166 INTERIOR WITH A VIOLIN 1917

167 Mauve Dress 1942

168 JEANNETTE I 1910   169 JEANNETTE II 1910

forehead and the distortion of the nose and mouth. With stage three *(Ill. 170)* realism has faded before expression conveyed by the swollen nature of certain features—eyes, nose, locks of hair—and by the alteration of certain dimensions by surfaces onto which the light falls.

While the first stage was sculpted in the presence of the model, the others were executed without her, and developed according to an independent logic; these bring to light all the potentialities contained in the initial interpretation. Their evolution derived from the tactile quality that Matisse considered essential to his sculpture; he used to explain how he would run his fingers over the model, take in its shape, and then transform the clay into an equivalent of the sensations he had received. In this case the sensations accentuate the mark of fingers in the clay and the sculpture no longer consists of a merely enveloping surface. *Jeannette IV (Ill. 171)* is moulded by violent movements, almost shredded by the pressures that separate the mass of hair into distinct clumps; the face is elaborated and the eyelids enlarged. A certain calm is re-established in the final stage *(Ill. 172)*, even though the mass of hair has given way to a larger forehead and nose, and though in an extraordinary equivalence, the left eye has been replaced by a protuberance carved along a plane.

171
JEANNETTE IV
1910–11 ?

170
JEANNETTE III
1910–1911

172
JEANNETTE V
1910–11 ?

173 STILL-LIFE WITH OYSTERS 1940

174 PINEAPPLE AND ANEMONES 1940

175 Reclining Nude II *c.* 1929

176 Seated Nude 1925

177 THE BACK I *c.* 1910   178 THE BACK II *c.* 1913

These two last versions are really expressionist in effect and extremely daring; they foreshadow the eloquent distortions which Picasso was to reach in his sculpture some years later.

With the large *The Back (Ills. 177–180)* now known in all its four successive versions, we are in the presence of what is surely the artist's major work in the field of sculpture. In fact he worked on it in stretches for twenty years, from approximately 1910 to 1930. It consists of a bas-relief two metres high, showing a single female figure from behind, her head leaning against her raised left arm and her right arm hanging down by her side. A reminder of the first study is preserved in an ink drawing of a strongly built model, heavily muscled and thick-set. The first stage *(Ill. 177),* a relatively realistic one, reflects the character of the model by accentuating her features, while the massive effect is increased still further by the fact that the feet do not appear at all, so that the body seems to be planted

179 THE BACK III *c.* 1916–17   180 THE BACK IV *c.* 1930

up to the ankles in the ground. Deeply engraved furrows mark the spine, and separate the planes of the shoulders, hip and loins. There is, perhaps, some slight resemblance to work by Maillol (who Matisse knew and visited) but a Maillol with its enveloping covering shattered.

The second stage *(Ill. 178)* exaggerates these fissures still more, literally carves up the surface, enlarges the limbs, joins the head and neck to the back, and makes the figure still more independent from the background by rendering this more animated. It gives the appearance of a rock wall out of which the body has been carved by using the natural ruggedness of the surface.

The third stage *(Ill. 179)* marks the abandonment of any human form for a genuinely architectural structure. The general curve in the form of an S of the preceding stages is attenuated in favour of the vertical orientation indicated by the massive pillars of the legs which

179

correspond to the right arm and the long plait of hair, both executed in a single movement and continued to below the narrowing of the waist. At the same time the proportions of the figure grow in relation to the whole, the left arm and head projecting above the upper edge of the sculpture.

This stage, which is still partially a compromise, finds its definitive expression in the last stage, *(Ill. 180)*. In this the dimensions taken on their final form, in one almost uninterrupted flow from top to bottom. Figure and background have blended together, no longer by accidental modelling, but in the calm of a pacified surface. The monumentality has reached its peak: this woman–column, henceforth more column than woman, is ready to be a confident support to the entablature of some temple of the modern age—a temple which has never yet been built.

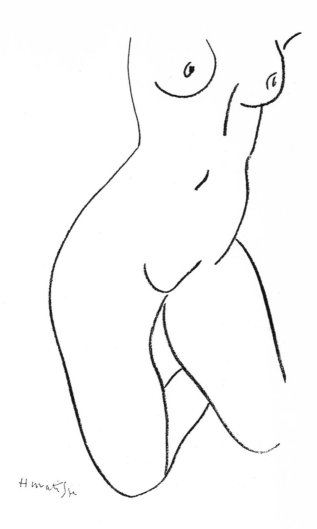

4 The World of Matisse

All artists measure themselves against the world, but of how many can it be said that they possess their own world ? One readily refers to the world of Bosch, Goya or Van Gogh. The same expression would hardly be used about Tiepolo, Van Dyck, or David, however magnificent their painting may have been. This is because the former were more than just painters: they were visionaries. What they saw did not coincide with their contemporaries' view, because they saw more, or better, or differently; and the way in which they perceived the world has been handed down to following generations. To a certain extent it has modified the present world. The true worth of an artist, his real originality can be assessed by this criterion.

This deeper vision expressed in a new form is the definition of creation, or rather, since nothing comes from nothing, re-creation: a mysterious operation, repeated again and again from the beginning. The artist plays an exceptional role in that he can prolong and modify the original creation, patiently perfect one of its innumerable possible, but rarely viable variations, until finally it can be adopted as it stands by others. What one can then detect in the work is the sum of dissimilarities which together make up this 'resemblance to itself' in which is born the total unity. To be unlike banal reality; to be like itself. This is the measure of a true artistic creation, and the previous chapter is ample illustration of the fact that it applies to the work of Matisse.

I shall now set out to map the world of Matisse, list its different elements, and examine its internal life. It is a world organized around a few clearly-defined central themes, which he dealt with again and again during his life, whether separately or together, and which remained a remarkably permanent feature.

182 Idol 1942

The first really major theme, which recurs frequently, is that of the human body. 'What interests me most,' the artist stated, 'is not still–lifes, or landscapes, but the human form. It is here that I can best express the almost religious feeling that I have about life.'

It was almost always a female figure. Apart from a few exceptions —male models in the Académie Carrière, musicians, Moroccans— women haunt Matisse's universe. They inhabit it in a still more sovereign way than in Renoir's or Degas' canvases. Renoir treated them as beautiful living fruit whose skin effectively caught the light; while Degas saw them as some sort of superior animals surprised at their toilet, or their exercises. Matisse's women do nothing; they do not even move. They are completely engrossed in simply being women, as entirely and magnificently as they can, that is to say in luxury and idleness. At the very most they may be reading, playing some musical instrument (piano or guitar) or engaged in the pleasures of conversation. But they are usually absorbed in idle day–dreams

183 CONVERSATION 1941

or more simply in the consciousness of their own beauty, (for instance one canvas called, significantly, *Idol*, *Ill. 182*). Beauty triumphs in its nudity, and also pleases in the elegance of dresses, hats, plumes or in the oriental costume of the odalisques. There is a strong flavour of the east in Matisse's conceptions ·of woman, passive and admired, always ready for pleasure.

Even when he grew older Matisse remained very sensitive to female beauty, and a pronounced sensuality emanated from his nudes, especially those which reclining among cushions and flowers seem to be caressed by each curve of the line. 'Women are grown–up children,' he said, 'they are the children of man's desire, and of his passion. But this passion is not reflected in them; it remains in the painter's mind, and consequently in the spectator's. Nothing can shatter the eternal serenity of their pose or appearance. Impassive and immobile, they keep their own secrets and remain themselves.' By becoming a painting a woman becomes in some way the painter's

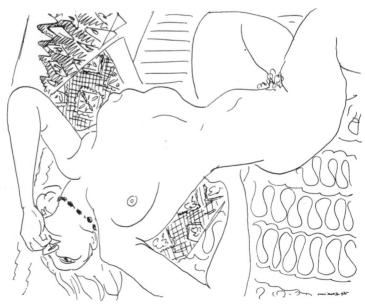

186
DANCER SITTING
IN AN ARMCHAIR
1942

187
DANCER IN
A BLUE TUTU
1942

188
THE READER,
MARGUERITE MATISS[
1906

189
MARGUERITE
READING
c. 1906

child, a part of him. Just as Flaubert said: 'Madame Bovary, *c'est
moi*', Matisse might have echoed: 'I am each of my models'. This
is what gives them all a certain kinship, whether reclining, day-
dreaming or leaning against a window-sill. They are the imagination
and the dream of the artist in many different forms.

The portraits are naturally rather different; most important

190
MADAME MATISSE
IN RED MADRAS
1907–8

among them are the numerous studies of Matisse's wife and daughter Marguerite *(Ills. 188–190)*. The familiarity of their personalities resists annexation, and there is a continual respect for their character and their identity throughout the artist's different periods.

The complete list of portraits painted or drawn by Matisse during his lifetime would be very long: portraits of members of his family (his daughter Marguerite, *Ills. 188–9*), of close friends, painters (Marquet, Derain), writers (Montherlant, Léautaud, Aragon, Ehrenburg), musicians (Prokofiev), doctors (Professor Leriche), faithful collectors from his early years (Miss Cone, *Ill. 193*, Sarah and Michael Stein, *Ill. 192*, Shchukin, *Ill. 191*), fashionable women (Baroness Gourgaud, Princess Galitzine), to which must be added the many self-portraits *(Ill. 194)* done at various periods of his life.

These portraits are valuable not for superficial exactness of reproduction, but for the profound truth they reflect. The incidental lines of the features, the local geography of the model, disappear in

191
PORTRAIT OF
SERGE SHCHUKIN
1912

192
PORTRAIT OF
SARAH STEIN
1916

193
PORTRAIT OF
CLARIBEL CONE
1933

194
SELF-PORTRAIT
WITH A STRAW HAT
1941

195
PORTRAIT OF CORTOT
1926

favour of a secondary resemblance based on the architecture of the face. The simplification of lines and dimensions does not make them vulgar caricatures, which exaggerate a particular feature at the expense of the others; these portraits seek out, as if from within, a characteristic merely suggested by the visible lines. This emerged only as a result of frequent meetings between painter and model and in the course of several sessions.

The first would be devoted to a preliminary study in charcoal. Matisse described his method of working in a book of reproductions of some hundred of his portraits: 'After half an hour, or an hour, I am surprised to see appear on my paper little by little a more or less precise picture resembling the person I am drawing.

196 Michaela 1943

'The likeness comes to me as if each charcoal line were clearing from a mirror the steam which prevents me from seeing my model.'

Gradually, from one sitting to the next, 'the most important features, the living substance of the work' detach themselves, as a result of 'an emotional understanding which makes me realize the warmth of the person's heart; this will result in a painted portrait, or in the possibility of expressing in rapid sketches what I have absorbed of the model'. Then revealed are, 'visions, which while appearing fairly superficial, are in fact the expression of an intimate relationship between the artist and his model. Drawings containing all the subtleties of observations made during the sessions burst forth in bubbles of fermentation, as if from a pool.' The final result is thus the projection of a person in Matisse's mind, and finally the balance of his relationship with the model, who in this way is doubly personified.

197 Seated Odalisque 1928

198 TAHITIAN LANDSCAPE 1930

Apart from in his portraits, Matisse rarely painted an isolated figure in a canvas. His people demanded a setting, and, as the years went by, the surroundings were magnified and became increasingly important *(Ill. 196)*. Carpets or materials provide not merely an incidental background, but also a suitably sensuous setting for the delicacy of a woman. Bunches of flowers laid around her are like offerings to her beauty. In the later pictures large plants with green leaves, creepers and palms close in all around her; their curves echo those of her body. In the gouache cut-outs, all difference of texture abolished, their pure rhythms are completely unified to those of the bather or diver. The identification is complete.

Animals, on the other hand, play no part. Despite the fact that Matisse had dogs, cats and entire aviaries of birds, these very rarely figure in his work apart from the occasional dove or swan. An unexpected exception is made for goldfish; their vermilion scales enliven many compositions, they are alive and silent presences floating in transparent water which reflects leaves and plants *(Ill. 69)*.

Straightforward landscapes were never Matisse's favourite subjects. Certainly some do exist, and admirable ones at that; but they are fewer than works on other themes. When young, the artist was often tempted by a particular subject. At Belle-Ile or in Corsica, he was drawn by the sight of the sea, or the light playing in the olives *(Ill. 24)*. When he moved into his rooms on the Quai Saint-Michel he painted many studies of historic surroundings seen from the window of his studio: Notre-Dame *(Ill. 12)*, the embankments of the Seine, the Louvre *(Ill. 25)*. Their historical nature did not prevent Matisse from subordinating their appearance to the laws of his plastic experiences. When he was living on the edge of the Clamart woods he used to treat the trees and paths through the forest in the same way *(Ill. 74)*; and also, to a still greater extent, the intense harmonies of Saint-Tropez *(Ill. 29)* and Collioure *(Ills. 34-5)*, which he combined with the mystical charm of Moroccan gardens *(Ill. 58)*. All of them were subjects which related to his journeys, but he only used those in which he recognised some element of himself. Unlike his friend Marquet, who painted every port in Europe, Matisse did not travel in order to broaden his horizon. From his visit to Tahiti he brought back only a few drawings

199
ROCKING–CHAIR,
TAHITI
1930

200
RED STUDIO
1911

201
LARGE
STILL-LIFE
WITH AUBERGINES
1911-12

202 LARGE RED INTERIOR 1948

(Ills. 198-9); his impressions emerged later in the form of plants and palms, but without any of Gauguin's exoticism. The few views of the shore and cliffs at Etretat were the result of short summer holidays away from Nice, and are merely the diversions of an adopted southerner beguiled in passing by the freshness of the north.

Painted only rarely for their own sake, landscapes came into Matisse's work, once could almost say, by the window. Framed in the rectangle of a casement window *(Ills. 34 and 61)*, the countryside is present without being obvious, at once close and distant, both visible and secondary, rather as in a play. In the Nice canvases, in particular, one or two palm trees, standing between sea and sky, are often sufficient to evoke it.

Matisse's favourite surroundings were always interiors. Not the closed and cosy interiors of the north, which gather around the warmth of the hearth. Nor the comfortable rooms, draped with curtains, lit up by lamps scattered everywhere, which were so beautifully evoked by Bonnard or Vuillard. On the contrary, his interiors are open, welcoming, sometimes even anonymous (he lived much of his life in hotels). They are interiors of the south, at once insulated against the sun and allied to it *(Interior with Violin, Ill. 166)*. The particular value of the shutters can be seen in the play of sunlight filtering into the room *(Ills. 83 and 203-4)*; this has been perceptively analysed by André Rouveyre:

'Shutters have always been important elements in Matisse's scenes. They appear in his canvases both as a mobile factor and as a boundary line between public and private worlds. It is here that, for him, the sharp arrows of sunlight come to break, melt, fade or insinuate themselves. It is here that begins the field of his spiritual and visual sensualities, his thoughtful emotions, his colour concertos... Shutters are for Matisse, as a painter of interior intimacy, what the parasol is in the wilds of the countryside. With this, and more effectively than Joshua with his trumpet, he is the lord of the sun.'

The painter himself, speaking of the Hôtel de la Méditerranée in Nice, recalled with evident pleasure, 'the light that came through the shutters. It came from below like theatre footlights' *(Mauve Dress, Ill. 167)*.

203
LARGE INTERIOR,
NICE
1921

204
WOMAN ON
A DIVAN
1922

205 ASIA 1946

206
INTERIOR
WITH AN
EGYPTIAN
CURTAIN
1948

The still-lifes are also fragments of interiors: they are often not limited to a collection of objects on a table, but include the surrounding space *(Ills. 174, 206* and *212)*. They would not bear Matisse's particular stamp if they were only reproductions of an arrangement of furniture or objects. The passive accumulation of his early years was soon replaced by a careful choice of objects, a chamber concerto like a Cézanne, but with greater freedom and without his ingrained obstinacy.

207
GOURDS
1916

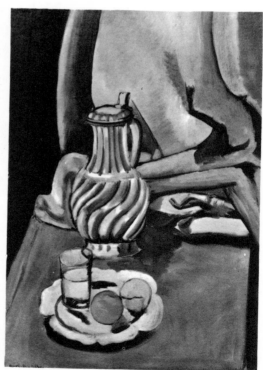

208
PEWTER JUG
1916–17

209
TULIPS AND OYSTERS
1943

210
LEMONS AND PEWTER JUG
1939

211 LEMONS AND MIMOSA ON A BLACK BACKGROUND 1944

As Matisse explained to his pupils: 'When it comes to still–lifes, the painting consists of colouring the objects chosen by the artist for his composition, taking into account the different qualities of the tones and their relationships...

'Copying the objects which make up a still–life is nothing. What matters is to express the feeling they inspire in you, the emotion that the whole composition arouses, the harmonies between the different objects, and the specific nature of each of them, modified by its harmonies with the others. The whole thing is knotted together like a rope or a snake...

'A still–life is as difficult to reproduce as an antique. The proportions of the different objects which make it up, their dimensions and their colours are as important as the proportions of the head or hands of, for example, Greek or Roman sculptures.'

The preliminary choice of elements in a still–life gives it a certain atmosphere. Oudry's poultry, Van Gogh's large shoes, Chardin's peaches, or Braque's grapes are unique to them. Matisse's fruit is more often oranges and lemons *(Ill. 210)*, painted in a very delicate yellow against black marble, or perhaps pineapples. Instead of the over-transparent glass exploited by the Dutch, he prefers plain pottery, vases with bold curves, or a peasant pewter jug enlivening the bare surfaces of a table or cloth *(Ill. 208)*. All flowers are welcome, from the fresh wild flowers to anemones *(Ill. 174)*, magnolia, geraniums, saxifrage, gladioli, or fragile white Christmas roses.

Matisse was very fond of tapestries, mottled eastern carpets, materials with large floral designs: *(Large Still-life with Aubergines*, 1911–12, *Ill. 201)*. Their pronounced patterns do not interfere with each other, with the unity of the canvas, or with the con-

212
STILL–LIFE
1946

tours of the objects. On the contrary, both are mutually enhanced, and the multiple combination of tiles, checked patterns and stripes produces a similar effect. Quite apart from their plastic value, the relationship between the objects and the painter, has been called emotional; Matisse always refused to eat any of the food which he had painted.

The presence of familiar objects which appear again and again is not unwise because they do not feature as such, but only in terms of their properties of inspiration. Thus a certain Arab tapestry, which hung in his studio, was the pretext of ten different pictures. As Matisse explained: 'The object is not so very interesting in itself. It is the surroundings that create it. I have worked all my life in front of the same objects, they convince me of reality and make me reflect on what they have gone through for me and with me. A glass of water with a flower is a different thing from a glass of water with a lemon. The object is an actor: a good actor can act in ten different plays, an object can play a different role in ten different pictures. It is never considered alone, but evokes a host of elements... About this table that I painted isolated in a garden? Well, that represented a whole outdoor environment in which I have lived.'

In the same way the musical instruments which feature so frequently, guitars, violins, harmoniums, pianos are equally representative of a musical atmosphere. They are, perhaps, symbols of the music of form, the song of colours which Matisse tirelessly took up again and again throughout his career *(Ills. 213-4)*.

The role played by reality in Matisse's world is revealed by two remarks of his. 'I do not paint things,' he said once, 'I paint the difference between them.' When somebody said that the painter did not see women as he painted them; he replied, 'If I met women like them in the street, I should be appalled. I do not create a woman,

214
PIANO LESSON
1923

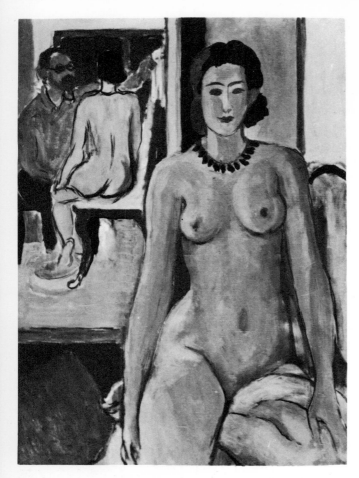

I paint a picture.' This corollary can be added: 'If one painted portraits so accurate and so real that they gave the illusion of nature
and appeared alive, and then decorated the walls of a room with
them, the result would be atrocious and so obsessive that the spectator would eventually flee.'

The force of expression of the work thus transcends the rights of
reality. Nature is no longer a dictionary, as it was to Delacroix, but
a text to translate into another language, something implicit and
absolute out of which a different order is elaborated, not in contradiction to it, but ever preponderant over it. Transposition is not a
liberty, but a duty.

Two signs of this preponderance can be detected. The first is the frequent presence of the painter himself in his work, part of his body: his hand holding the brush, for example; and once, in his youth, he drew his feet into the foreground of a scene. Often it is his face which appears, reflected in a mirror at the back of the scene: an alert face, watching the model and watching himself *(Ills. 215-6)*. In this way, the importance of the creator in his creation is asserted; neither drawing nor picture could be confused with an anonymous reflection of reality. Even an inattentive observer could not help but realize that they did not just appear like a snapshot. It is thus a reminder of the fact that the subject does not exist in its own right, and that it has no autonomy. It becomes what the painter wishes it to be.

The other, even more eloquent sign can be found in Matisse's use of his own works as decoration in later canvases. This deliberate way of introducing pictures, drawings or sculptures of his own in other pictures or drawings (many examples could be cited from the interiors of 1896 to his last canvases in 1948), remains a very characteristic stamp of Matisse's work. Works reproduced in this

216 NUDE BY A MIRROR 1937

way are sometimes hidden behind other objects, or cut off by the edge of the canvas. At times they create rhythms with other forms. Sometimes they are arranged in what amounts to an exhibition; in *Red Studio (Ill. 200)* there are some twelve canvases, (among them *Young Sailor* and the second version of *Luxury*), sculptures and ceramics scattered around a studio, in which the walls, as well as the floor, the furniture and the table cloth are all a uniform red. In this general tonality of strong red, the colour variations provided by the canvases, their original colours modified by the dominant red, have an increased effect and the result is exceptionally striking.

The references to earlier works were not caused by complacency or conceit. Possibly Matisse found it hard to abandon certain works which were particularly dear to him (for instance *Luxury* and *The Dance*). His affection for these was certainly genuine, and perhaps this was a way of prolonging his work on them. But there is more to this sort of secondary creation: a means of suggesting, in a new form, a certain ambiguity of reality, a cleverly calculated uncertainty between the thing or the person and its image. A very subtle uncertainty exists, for example, in the case of *Piano Lesson (Ill. 73)*, where the figure of a woman on a stool, in fact a painting *(Ill. 66)* hung on the wall, seems at first sight to be a living person, presiding over the child's piano exercises. This is the way Matisse showed that things are unattached and easily slip from reality into the world of painting and *vice versa*. In *Large Red Interior (Ill. 202)* the table in the left-hand corner of the canvas is reproduced with no greater degree of realism than the one with the pineapple on it in the picture on the right wall, and the pineapple itself has no less presence than the lemons on the table. In the same way the plant in the black drawing hung on the left wall, is no less a plant than the bunches of flowers which litter the room. The drawing and the painting are not windows opened out of the wall, and add no second perspective to the interior, but they are an inherent part of the whole, of the different levels of the canvas, where a continuing and perfectly coherent space is suggested. This transposed reality and the repetition of his earlier work are a unique pictorial statement.

The women, flowers and objects chosen by Matisse and recreated, transmuted by him, change substance while loosing nothing of their presence. In one sense the word 'ease' can be used. Far from multiplying the defences or the keys, the artist made access to the meaning of his works as simple as possible. Aragon said that to find an equivalent of this 'ease' of Matisse's, one should look for it in the work of a musician, in particular Bach. The comparison is naturally only of the means, but it is a revealing one. Is the purity of the music opposed to the richness of the notes ? Behind an outward appearance of ease, obviousness, even at times neglect, because the work retains the spontaneity of a sketch or improvisation, Matisse is nonetheless an able architect. If this is not obvious, it is because he had the elegance to efface the traces of his work and calculations, to remove from his construction every minute reminder of the scaffolding that served to build it. Just as Racine can seem less 'constructed' than Flaubert, and a cunning curve less 'architectural' than a geometric construction with carefully calculated angles.

'My curves are not mad !' Matisse was careful to explain. He might have added: 'My colours are not drunk.' This was, in effect, what he did say hundreds of times, as when, after saying: 'I have a great love for pure, clear, sparkling colour and I am always surprised to find beautiful colours dulled and dirtied unnecessarily,' he went on to explain: 'A great modern victory is that the secret of *expression rendered by colour* has been found.'

This brings us to the inevitable subject of decoration. It has often been said, sometimes with hostile overtones, that Matisse's art is merely decorative, meaning by this that it is superficially agreeable form, pleasing to the eye, and neglects any deeper meaning. This criticism is one that has often been used in connection with any art form which has a perfect clarity in the drawing, adopts a simplified expression and above all makes use of essentially pleasing colours. Typically enough this criticism is never made when the colours are dark or grey even if their design is simple. Matisse's answer to this reproach, which he heard many times was as follows: 'Delacroix used to say, "We are not understood, we are merely accepted".' Decoration is an extremely valuable element in a work of art. It is an essential quality. It is therefore not pejorative to say that an artist's paintings are decorative. All French primitives are decorative.

Participation in life is a characteristic of modern art. A picture in a room radiates happiness by its colours, which should soothe us.

Naturally these colours are not scattered around unthinkingly, but arranged in an expressive fashion. A picture on a wall should be like a bunch of flowers in a room.

Expressed in this way, decoration, far from being a minor attribute, condescendingly tolerated, becomes an added force, a supreme glow, like a smile. There is no need to see emptiness in a smile; instead, it could be a mark of successful effort—as a dancer smiles at the most strenuous moment of her dance—or a sign of the achievement of serenity in wisdom. Matisse's painting is indeed decorative, in the same way as primitives, eastern miniatures, Romanesque frescoes, and stained-glass windows are. It is in tune with the contemporary sensitivity which it has absorbed completeiy.

Decoration, thus defined, presupposes the presence of a particular light. 'In my art,' Matisse said, 'I have tried to create a crystalline atmosphere for the mind. I found the required limpidity in several parts of the world, in New York, in the South Seas, and in Nice.' It is a limpidity from which shadows are barred, and, because the light had dispersed the shadows, it is important when really investigating Matisse's world to be aware of what is excluded.

Most obviously, Matisse has banished chance. The fortuitous delights of matter were not of interest to someone who said how little attracted he was by the drawings on old walls, the imprecise suggestions of raw material and the informal. Substances acquire dignity only when submitted to the intellect. But a work of art must be free from all haphazard encounters. The phrase attributed to Courbet, which states that an artist must be capable of starting a real masterpiece again from the beginning to prove that when he did it he was not merely a plaything of emotion or chance, haunted

218
DECORATIVE FIGURE
ON AN ORNAMENTAL
BACKGROUND
1927

Matisse for a long time, and was instrumental in making him set his standards as high as he did.

Above all he wanted to see everything with absolute clarity. He led and would not be led, except by his judgment and intelligence. Thus the obscure forces of the irrational were also excluded. Matisse stood at the opposite pole from surrealism; no realist, he insisted passionately on the need to be conscious. He had no visions, since he used all his energy in perfecting his single vision, so clear, so free that it cast into obscurity (in the shadow which does not exist, since even black is light) everything which did not possess an intelligible form, everything that was undefined. He reduced the monsters of the subconscious to silence.

Consequently, evil too was banned. Matisse was the antithesis of his friend Rouault. He was not unaware of the existence of misery, war, sin and ugliness; but he denied and rejected them. His art was not created as compensation for them, but in absolute opposition to them. He was already part of the world beyond faults and forgiveness, that of paradise regained. Perhaps his approach is Oriental in this respect: he evokes an earthly paradise of his own, an ideal place for the mind to go when it has reached ultimate wisdom, without repudiating terrestial splendours.

At the same time we must guard against thinking that this serenity was achieved without cost, that this happiness came of its own accord. Matisse has too often been reduced to the status of a purveyor of 'the joy of living', a mere distiller of carefree pleasures. Just as his apparent ease and facility are the fruit of endless research and questioning, his tranquillity must not be confused with placidity, however cerebral.

As he said to Père Couturier: 'They say that my work comes from the mind. This is not true: everything that I have done has been done from passion.' No one has shown up better this mysterious quality than Jean Bazaine, when he asked: 'Lucidity, purity in Matisse? The man who invented fauvism, who all his life drew these faces, these flowers, these quivering nudes, whose clarity of form is won at such a cost of dark and doubtful battles, of mastered violence, who painted the walls of the Vence chapel with such profoundly tragic signs—I think that this man can teach us again how dearly bought is "the beautiful French painting, so bright..."

as Renoir called it. In France "clarity" has been a confused notion (just as there is confusion over the word tragedy) ever since the key to it was thought to lie in dull painting and equivocation. Matisse's dominating passion is evident in his every line, just as Cézanne's baroque violence shows through his classical construction or Philippe de Champaigne's sensitive strength from under his hair shirt: clear form is not given.'

Examples of Matisse's passion, which at times borders on aggression, are not lacking: for instance *Gypsy (Ill. 220)* is a typical work of the fauve period in the violence of its colours and syncopation of its lines. The form is lacerated, tortured. The reds and greens have the brutality of blows inflicted on the woman's body, from which all softness has been effaced by her savage excitement. The pure vermilion outlines around her eyes, arms and bust evoke wounds rather than the gentle warmth of shadows, and Matisse's treatment of the face rivals Soutine, or even Karel Appel in its tortured intensity.

Such a display of passion was not limited to Matisse's fauve period. Certain drawings of the 1950s show an equal degree of intensity though in a different style. It is difficult to believe at first sight that one nude *(Ill. 219)* was by the same hand as the many little odalisques. The blurred charcoal outline bears the trace of dozens of earlier lines, which gradually sacrificed flexibility and sinuosity in a dramatic search for a jerky rhythm, full of right angles, stressed and rigid lines. They express neither grace nor voluptuousness, but distress, the solitude of a human being reduced to a mere dislocated puppet, and the precariousness of the human condition, with as much strength as Picasso and, no doubt, less rhetoric.

The ultimate tragedy of Christ's passion is portrayed in the *Stations of the Cross* at Vence *(Ill. 221)*. The message comes across all the clearer in the great violent lines, in the complete lack of curves, harmony of contour, or 'decoration' of any kind. It is a message of violence. There is no room for virtuosity, nor indeed 'beauty'. This concern for expression alone is entirely justified by the subject.

The word 'pagan' has often been used about Matisse, at least before the Vence chapel. His accusers should have asked themselves whether there is no form of spiritualism in paganism. In the case of

Matisse's more carnal creations, what strikes one is that he was able to transcend voluptuousness so perfectly by a vision of plenitude culminating in a form of 'Oriental' mystical insight. The dominant, liberated sensation already belongs to the plane of eternal values, that he insisted on preserving. After talking of his 'almost religious' feeling about life, he stressed to Père Couturier that his religious feeling never left his work, 'not even the Odalisques'.

Between this respect for the sacred character of every living thing and a properly Christian conviction there is nonetheless a great gap, which no one would have dreamt Matisse was capable of crossing before the first plans for the chapel. A few years before, the artist had written in his text for *Jazz*: 'Do I believe in God? Yes, when I am working, when I am modest and submissive, I feel myself to be greatly guided by someone who leads me to create things which are

219
KNEELING NUDE
1950

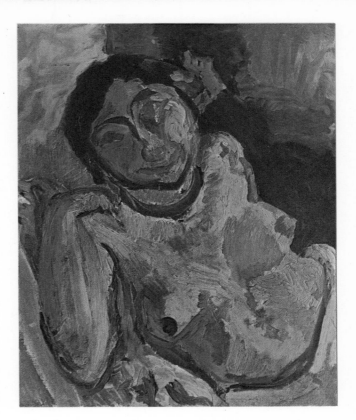

220
GYPSY
1905–6

beyond me.' But a scruple obliged him to continue: 'However, I
do not feel grateful towards Him, because it is as if I were in the
presence of a conjuror whose tricks I cannot understand. I feel
deprived of the benefits of experience, which should have been the
reward for my efforts. I am ungrateful, and unashamedly so.'

During the building of Notre-Dame du Rosaire, contradictory
evidence about Matisse's beliefs was provided by his friends,
whether atheists, Catholics or priests. André Verdet said that the
painter's only religion was that of love for the work being created.
But several times he admitted to Couturier that he had resorted to
prayer, and derived comfort from it. On the other hand, nothing
enables one to speak of a conversion in the precise sense of the term.
Neither has one any authority to doubt Matisse's sincerity, on the way
in which his emotions were coloured by the influence of the
Christian themes that he was dealing with. (One is reminded of the

221
THE FIFTH
STATION OF
THE CROSS,
Notre-Dame
du Rosaire,
Vence,
1947–51

sceptic Delacroix who was inspired by religious chants while he was working on his frescoes in Saint-Sulpice.)

The authenticity of the religious atmosphere of the Vence chapel, considered quite apart from its author, cannot be questioned, unless one identifies fervour with obscurity, meditation with a Romanesque nave or a Gothic pointed arch, and thinks of religious art as being inseparable from the traditional forms of the past. When the mystery is that of Christ, one runs no risk of weakening it by exposing it to the stark clarity of day. One must not forget either that the sanctuary was designed for an enclosed monastic community, and more precisely for an order of nuns. It suggests that the incantation in honour of woman, formulated in almost all Matisse's work, was finally sublimated into this gift to women consecrated to God without losing the essence of its meaning. Its religious quality may also lie in the calm tranquillity in which the mind remains vigilant in the silence and worship of beauty. It is rather like the sacred nature of the Canticles or the Song of Solomon, a wager on the happiness of the chosen and the clarity of Paradise.

5 After his Death

223 BLACK DOOR 1942

24 THE LIVED-IN SILENCE OF HOUSES 1947

Matisse himself exhausted all his own theories by working out the ultimate logical conclusions of each of them. This explains why one cannot speak of successors, as such, in Matisse's case. We saw how his one attempt at direct teaching rapidly came to an end and provoked this disillusioned remark: 'Nothing can be transmitted'.

There have certainly been inheritors only too eager to tame fauvism and reduce its savage proportions to the required standards set by the Salons. Marrying Matisse and Bonnard not unskilfully, they evolved an agreeable style of painting, iridescent and essentially pleasing, which found a reliable market among prudent buyers. But this cannot be counted.

The works of his last period, in appearance so elementary (for instance *Young English Girl*, *Ill. 226*) and consequently so easy to copy, were also to tempt a number of imitators. Matisse was only too aware of this danger when he wrote to the Curator of the Philadelphia Museum at the time of his retrospective exhibition in 1948: 'I ask myself whether this collection of my works will not have a bad influence on the young painters. How are they going to interpret the impression of apparent ease that they will receive after a rapid, superficial, glance at my canvases and drawings?

'I have always tried to conceal my efforts, I have always wanted my works to be as light and gay as spring, so that no one would ever guess the labour they demanded. Now I am afraid that young painters, seeing only the apparent easy and careless drawing, will use this as an excuse to do away with certain exercises that I believe to be necessary.

'The few exhibitions that I have had the occasion to see during these last years make me suspect that the young avoid the slow and painful preparation necessary to any contemporary painter, and claim instead to be able to construct with colours alone.'

225
Hɪɴᴅᴜ Pᴏsᴇ
1923

And so Matisse formulated this very basic warning: 'When an artist has not prepared for his maturity by a period of work which is only remotely connected with the final result, then he has little future; or when an artist who has "arrived" no longer sees the need for returning to the soil from time to time, he starts going round in circles, repeating himself indefinitely, until finally even his curiosity vanishes in this repetition.'

Finally he said: 'My ambition is not to teach. I do not want my exhibition merely to give rise to false interpretations in the minds of those who still have their future to carve out. I should like people to know that colour cannot be treated carelessly, and that strict preparation is necessary before one is worthy to use it.'

While nothing is to be said for mere imitation of Matisse, it cannot be denied that he has deeply influenced others ever since his early years. We saw to what extent his personality dominated all his friends as early as the heroic period of fauvism, and how much people like Derain, Dufy, and Camoin owe to him. The painters who flocked to Paris from all over the world, at the beginning of the century, sensed it too. Among them, Germans and Russians came in the greatest number: Caspar and Jawlensky arrived in 1905, Kandinsky in 1906, Franz Marc in 1903, Paula Modersohn-Becker came several times after 1900, Nolde himself as early as 1888 (the date of his meeting with Signac). The movement christened *Die Brücke* (the Bridge) which developed in Dresden between 1905 and 1911, centred mainly around Kirchner and Schmidt-Rottluff, has been considered to be a German version of fauvism looking towards Munch and Nolde. The violence of their colours underlined the expression of form. Many analogies between Kirchner, the strongest personality of the group, and Matisse have been drawn (Matisse was eleven years younger) and at times it has even been suggested that Kirchner might have antedated some of his works so as to stress his independence. On several occasions during the last few years their works have been shown together and the public has been able to draw its own conclusions. Such joint exhibitions include: 'The European Fauves' in Schaffhausen and Berlin, 1959; 'The Sources of Modern Art' in Paris, 1960–1961; 'French Fauvism' and

227 SLEEPING WOMAN 1936

the 'Beginning of German Expressionism' in Paris and Munich, 1966.

Certainly Matisse's three stays in Germany between 1908 and 1910, his private exhibition organized by the dealer Cassirer in Berlin (1908-1909), and the translation of his statements about art into German and Russian all had great repercussions among young artists, some of whom went to his Paris academy, where the Bavarian Hans Purrmann took an active part.

In Munich, another of the most active art centres, the seeds of fauvism were introduced by Jawlensky and Kandinsky, both Russians, who had lived in France and shown canvases in the Salon d'Automne in 1905. Kandinsky's figurative and intensely coloured work, done during his stay in Murnau, preceded the foundation of the *Blaue Reiter* movement and its transition into abstraction. In the very heart of this movement Kandinsky developed and submitted to the geometry of dancing forms the strength of colour which he had earlier unleashed in his landscapes and figures.

Bernard Dorival pointed to French fauvism's rapid and important diffusion across Germany, remarking that fauve canvases were shown in Munich by the N.K.V.M. in 1910, in Berlin (Secession, *Der Sturm* and *Blaue Reiter*), in 1911, 1912 and 1913, in Cologne (Sonderbund) in 1912. Matisse had another private exhibition in Berlin in 1913.

At about the same time the fauves were also spreading to other countries: Alfred Stieglitz devoted an exhibition to Matisse alone as early as 1908, and then in 1910 and 1912 showed him in his New York gallery. Works by various members of the group were exhibited in the famous 'Armory Show' in New York, Chicago and Boston in 1913. In England, Brighton had shown some canvases in 1910, London in 1910, 1911 and 1912 (Grafton Gallery and Doré Gallery), in Russia, St Petersburg and Moscow in 1912, in Switzerland, Zurich, in Belgium (Brussels and Ghent) in 1912, and in Denmark, Copenhagen in 1914.

Even cubism, once it had transcended its period of analytical austerity devoted to quasi-monochrome constructions, betrayed, when the time came for it to turn to pure colour, a debt to Matisse. If one studies their origins carefully, Delaunay's orphism, Léger's violent contrasts, and even Italian futurism are not absolutely free

228
Illustration for
Poésies
by Mallarmé 1932

229
Pablo Picasso
Head of a Girl

of his influence. And as for Picasso, long considered to be as opposed to Matisse as the south pole is to the north, some of his elegant and fluid line drawings, dominating the white paper, reveal a quite unexpected affinity.

Finally, during the period of general questioning of traditional values in painting that took place between 1940 and 1950, when young painters took up their positions and named their true masters, they turned to Matisse, among a very small number of others (just as the fauves once turned to Cézanne, Van Gogh or Gauguin), because they were unable to tackle the problems of colour and space without taking into consideration Matisse's discoveries. Whether figurative or not, whether young or not so young (the American abstract painter Mark Rothko was fifty-one when he painted his *Homage to Matisse*, dated 1954, the year of the master's death), their ambition to push coloured expression to its ultimate registers corresponded to Matisse's late work and mainly to his large gouache cut-outs (such as *Snail, Ill. 137*). There was yet another revelation for the younger generation at the Kunsthalle exhibition at Berne in 1959, and at the one at the Musée des Arts décoratifs, Paris, in 1961.

If one now tries to assess Matisse's general position by placing him in the main currents of the history of art, one does not have to look far for his ancestors. However close his affinities may have been at certain times with the east, with Byzantium or Islam, there is no question that he belongs to the great French tradition that has its origins in Romanesque art. As the critic Bazaine puts it: 'The voluptuous Matisse is closer to the Middle Ages than to Fragonard's century. The breath that inspired the figures of *The Dance* is related to the sacred wind that brought, eight centuries earlier, the figures of the Saint-Savin vaults, the anonymous masters of Tavant or Nohant-Vicq. He rediscovered—without meaning to—the compact style, the violent and well-embodied lyricism, this sort of continual explosion of form.'

The Romanesque fresco and stained-glass artists immortalized the intense glow of colour-light and the patient illuminators in their monastic workshops, creators of a major and essentially 'fauve' style of painting, belong to that tradition, which, having almost vanished for two centuries, reappeared under different forms with Chardin, Delacroix, Manet, Gauguin and Cézanne. Its apogee lies in a certain marriage of grace and strength, passion and courtesy, an innate nobility which expresses itself only in a smile. Beauty is not considered to be a gift from heaven but a reward for endless patience and tenacious efforts. It cannot be separated from the quest for perfection of form. It is a product of the very soil of France.

6 Collections and Books

Matisse's works can be found in many museums and private collections across the entire world, but mainly in the United States of America, the USSR and France. Without going into details of enumeration which are beyond the scope of this study, it is nevertheless possible to give a rough outline of the resources of the different countries.

The wealth of works by Matisse in public museums in the United States is due above all to the fact that American art lovers were among the first to take an interest in him, and that their collections, as a result of total or partial donations, have gradually become public property. Many of the works collected by the Stein family have been dispersed, although certain major elements have been kept together in such museums as the Sarah and Michael Stein Memorial Collection in the San Francisco Museum of Art, which includes *Portrait of Sarah Stein, Ill. 192.* On the other hand the outstanding legacy of Etta Cone has endowed the Baltimore Museum of Art with about sixty paintings and bronzes and more than a hundred drawings, making up the Cone Collection. This is mainly centred around the period from 1905-1922 (*Blue Nude* [*Souvenir de Biskra*], *Ill. 161, Pewter Jug, Ill. 208, White Turban,* Etretat landscapes, interiors and odalisques of the Nice period, *Girl in Yellow, Ill. 96, Blue eyes, Ill. 99, Pink Nude, Ill. 100*).

Next on the list for the number and quality of the Matisses comes the Art Institute of Chicago (*Still-life with Geranium Plant and Fruit, Apples, Woman on a Rose Divan, Woman before an Aquarium*), the Museum of Modern Art in New York (*Moroccans, Ill. 72, Red Studio, Ill. 200, Blue Window, Ill. 55, Piano Lesson, Ill. 73; Rose Marble Table;* and in the 'sculpture garden' of the museum the reliefs of *The Back I, II, III, IV, Ills. 177-180* are hung side by side), the Philadelphia Museum of Art (*Mlle. Yvonne Landsberg, Moorish Screen, Ill. 217*, and *Lady in Blue* from the Chester Dale Collection), the San Francisco Museum of Art (*Vase of Anemones, Corsican Landscape, Girl with Green Eyes*, from the Harriet Lane Levy Bequest).

After these must be mentioned the museums at Boston (*Carmelina, Ill. 27*), Buffalo (*Notre-Dame in the Late Afternoon, Ill. 12*), Cambridge, Harvard University (*Geraniums*), Cleveland (*Interior with Etruscan Vase*), Columbus (*Etretat, Roses*), Houston (*View of Collioure*), Minneapolis (*White Feathers, Ill. 5, Boy with the Butterfly Net*), Saint Louis (*Bathers with a Tortoise, Ill. 42*), Washington, National Gallery of Art and the Phillips Collection (*Studio, Quai Saint-Michel, Ill. 71, Interior with an Egyptian Curtain, Ill. 206, Plumed Hat, La Coiffure* and *Moorish Woman*), Worcester (*Dance of the Nuns*), the Metropolitan Museum of New York (water colours and drawings).

And at least one canvas can be found in museums at Dallas (*Ivy in Flower*, a large gouache cut-out); Denver (*Two Sisters*); Detroit (*Interior with Window, Ill. 75*); Honolulu (*Girl Reading*); Los Angeles (*Reclining Woman with Anemones*); New Haven (*Still-life with Torso*); Providence, Rhode Island School of Design (*Still-life with Bowl and Book*); Richmond; Rochester (*Girl with a Tricorne*); San Diego, California (*Bunch of Flowers*); Toledo (*Dancer Resting*); West Palm Beach (*Lorette, Two Rays*).

The Barnes Foundation at Merion, near Philadelphia, must particularly be taken into consideration. It has about a hundred Matisses, among them a number of very important ones (*The Joy of Living, Ill. 36, Still-life with Melon, Madame Matisse in Red Madras, Ill. 190, Still-life with a Blue Patterned Tablecloth, Ill. 11, Seated Man of Rif, Ill. 63, Music Lesson, Ill. 213*, a contemporary but quite different version of the one in the New York Museum of Modern Art— *Seated Moorish Woman Ill. 87*, etc.). Dr Barnes, possessor of an immense fortune acquired in the pharmaceutical industry, decided to house the outstanding collection of modern paintings that he had built up around Renoir, Cézanne, the impressionists, Soutine, Matisse, Rouault and Picasso in a foundation bearing his name. For many years it was extremely difficult to get permission to enter the Barnes Foundation, which opened in 1924, due to the Doctor's very individual views and his wary hostility towards many categories of art lovers. As we have seen, his enthusiasm for Matisse led him, in 1930, to commission the painter's decoration *The Dance*, *Ill. 98* for the main hall where his works were shown. When *The Dance* was being installed Dr Barnes even published a great tome on the *Art of Henri Matisse*. After his death in 1951, measures were taken to get the Foundation opened to the public, a procedure which resulted, ten years later, in the collection being opened two days a week, under certain conditions.

It is not possible to mention all the private collections in America which include works by Matisse. However some of them which generously and thoughtfully allow the public access to their treasures in temporary exhibitions must be mentioned in passing. In the city of New York alone one can cite in the first rank Mr Pierre Matisse, son of the painter, and a tireless organizer of many important exhibitions, (*Male Model*, *St Anne's Chapel*, *Green Skirt*, *Dream* have appeared in many of them), but also Mr and Mrs Lee A. Ault, Dr and Mrs Harry Bakwin (*The Artist and His Model*, *Ill. 85*), Mr and Mrs William A.M. Burden, Mrs Gilbert Chapman, Mr and Mrs Ralph F. Colin (*Guitarist*, *Green Gandoura Shirt*), Mrs Marcel Duchamp (*Dancer and Armchair*, *Black Background*, *Ill. 140*), Mr and Mrs Albert Lasker ('*Royal Tobacco*', *Pineapple and Anemones*, *Ill. 174*, *Idol*, *Ill. 182*), Mr Robert Lehman, Mrs Maurice Newton (*Michaela*, *Ill. 196*), Mr and Mrs W.S. Paley, Mr and Mrs Otto Preminger (*Interior with Black Ferns*), Mr Nelson A. Rockefeller, Paul Rosenberg and Co, Mr Sam Salz, Mr Donald S. Stralem (*Hindu Pose*, *Ill. 225*), Mr and Mrs John Hay Whitney (*Window at Collioure*), as well as the Alex Hillman Corporation (*Pineapple*), and the Joseph H. Hirschhorn Collection, which includes an important group of sculptures.

To this long list one can add, in Chicago, Mr Leigh B. Block (*Young Sailor*); Mr and Mrs Nathan Cummings (*Lemons on a Pewter Plate*); in Washington, Mrs Robert Woods Bliss (*Yellow Dress*, *Zorah*, *Ill. 59*); in Saint Louis, Mr and Mrs. Joseph Pulitzer (*Conservatory*, *Ill. 104*); in Lake Forest, Mr and Mrs Alfred Cowles; in Santa Monica, California, Mr and Mrs Gifford Phillips; in Palm Beach, Mr Leray W. Berdeau; in San Francisco, Mr and Mrs Walter A. Haas (*Woman in a Hat*, *Madame Matisse*, *Ill. 30*, *Sketch for The Joy of Living*); in Los Angeles, Mr and Mrs Norton Simon (*Odalisque with Mauve and White Striped Gown*, *Ill. 108*), Mr and Mrs William Goetz,

Mr and Mrs Sidney F. Brody (*Lute*); in Beverly Hills, Mr and Mrs Taft Schreiber.

Across the rest of the American continent a few Matisses can be seen in Montreal, Ottawa and Toronto in Canada, and in the Museu de Arte de São Paulo in Brazil (*Plaster Torso*).

The fact that the USSR is so exceptionally rich in Matisse's works is due to the perspicacity of two great collectors, Shchukin and Morozov. Not that this is the result of gifts or legacies, but of the nationalization of private collections during the revolution of 1917 when the treasures of contemporary art collected by these two men became the property of the state. These very remarkable collections contained fifty-three of Matisse's canvases, now split between the Hermitage in Leningrad and the Pushkin Museum in Moscow. They naturally belong to the period preceding 1914, which they represent with a homogeneity unequalled in the entire world. Apart from the large compositions such as *Dinner Table, Red Version, Ill. 48*, *The Artist's Family*, or *The Dance, Ill. 51* and *Music, Ill. 53* of 1909-10, they include the most crowded still-lifes of the same period (*Decanter and Red Carpet*, which is another version of the large *Still-life with Red Carpet, Ill. 124* in Grenoble, *Still-life in Venetian Red, Bronze and Fruit, Vase of Irises on a Dressing-table, Goldfish, Ill. 69*), the best pictures resulting from the painter's visits to Spain and Morocco (*Spanish Girl with Tambourine, Zorah Standing, Ill. 56, Standing Man of Rif, Moroccan Triptych* so called because Morozov hung *Window at Tangiers, Ill. 61, Entry to the Casbah*, and *Zorah on the Terrace, Ill. 64* together), as well as some important portraits like that of *Madame Matisse* (1913), *Ill. 65*, the result of more than a hundred sittings.

In Japan, the collection of Shojiro Ishibashi in the Bridgestone Gallery in Tokyo includes seven important canvases (including *Marguerite in a Striped Coat*, *Odalisque with Raised Arms*), and Matisse is represented in the Fukushima Collection, the Ohara Art Gallery in Kurashiki, and a few others.

In Scandinavia, Oslo possesses *Portrait of Marquet* and *Sculpture and Persian Vase* in the Nasjonalgalleriet, and four paintings (among which is *Blue Dress in an Ochre Armchair*) in the Sonja Henie-Niels Onstad Collection; also Stockholm (*Moroccan Landscape, Tangiers, Ill. 58*) and Göteborg (*White Plumes, Ill. 79*).

In Denmark it is again due to the generosity of a far-sighted art lover, Johannes Rump, that the Nationalmuseet in Copenhagen owns such a large number of Matisses given in 1928 at the same time as an important collection of works by French contemporary masters. The Museum today owns eighteen canvases (among them: *Pink Onions, Luxury II, Ill. 38, Interior with a Violin, Ill. 166, Green Blouse*), a large gouache cut–out (*Zulma, Ill. 131*), five sculptures and three drawings. In addition to this, in the same town the Statens Museum for Kunst has *Self–Portrait* and *Portrait with Green Streak, Ill. 117*, the Ordrupgaard Museum has one canvas (*Flowers and Fruit*) and the Ny Carlsberg Glyptothek a bronze.

In Germany, works of Matisse can be found in the museums at Bremen (*Lorette*), Cologne, Wallraf–Richartz Museum (*Seated Young Lady*), Essen (*Still–life with Asphodels, Ill. 40*), Frankfurt–am–Main (*Still–life in Blue*); Munich (*Still–life with a Geranium*), Stuttgart (*Dressing*). In Czechoslovakia Matisse is represented in Prague, in Yugoslavia in Belgrade (*Trees near Melun*).

In Switzerland, a few lovely and important canvases belong to the museums in Basle (*Still–life with Oysters, Ill. 173, Bank*), Berne (*Anemones*), Lausanne (*Still–life with Knife*), Zurich (*Margot*), but the private collections own still more: the collections of H. Seligmann in Basle (*Young Sailor in a Beret*), Rudolf Staechelin (*Madame Matisse with a Manila Shawl, Ill. 50*) and Professor Hans Hahnloser (*Pewter Jug, Lorette in a Pink Armchair, Ill. 76*) in Berne, Max Moos (*Narcissi and Fruit*) in Geneva, S. Rosengart (*Lemons and Saxifrages*) in Lucerne, Silvan Kocher in Soleure, G. Zumsteg and Buehrle (*Carnival in Nice*) in Zurich.

The same situation is repeated in Belgium where the Musées Royaux des Beaux–Arts de Belgique (*Still–life, Ill. 212*) have less to show than the collections of P. Dotremont (*Collioure, Young Girl before a Window*), G. Daelemans (*Nude with Pink Shoes*), Marcel Mabille (*Window*), all in Brussels, Roland Leten in Ghent, and Léon Duesberg at Soiron–Verviers (*Mauve Dress, Ill. 167*).

In Holland the Stedilijk Museum in Amsterdam (*Odalisque, Ill. 91*) must be mentioned, and in Italy the Mattioli (*Seated Woman*), and Jucker (*Odalisque on a Blue Divan*) Collections in Milan.

In Great Britain, Glasgow Art Gallery (*Pink Table–Cloth, Head of a Young Girl*), Oxford and a few other private collections—Royan

Middleton in Dundee (*Piano Lesson, Ill. 214*), Morton in Glasgow, Frank Stoop in London (*Naked Woman, Blue Nude*), Kessler (*Still-life*) Lord Berners, etc.—own some of Matisse's works, but none of them can compare with the eleven canvases in the Tate Gallery, London (*Trees near the Trivaux Pond, Ill. 74, Nude Study in Blue, Ill. 26, Reading Woman with Parasol, Inattentive Reader, Notre-Dame, Reclining Nude II, Nude on the Beach, Standing Model, Distracted Weaver, Snail, Ill. 137*), in particular the fairly recent acquisition of two portraits (*Derain* by Matisse and *Matisse* by Derain) testifies to the efforts taken by this museum to represent the chief fauve in a comprehensive way. Apart from several pieces of sculpture, the Tate Gallery is rightly proud of its now complete series of four variations of the large *The Back, Ills. 177–180*, shown in such a way as to draw particular attention to their monumental size.

Finally, one can journey across France following the public collections of the country from north down to the south in the very steps of the artist himself. The first stage would be Le Cateau-Cambrésis, near Cambrai, Matisse's native town, which he endowed two years before his death with a museum designed to gather together the traces of his early work. Situated on the first floor of the Hôtel de Ville, this museum has no less than seventy-five works, but its nature explains why apart from two canvases (of which one is a copy of a Chardin) and a tapestry, it is essentially constituted by drawings, mostly of his earliest youth, nudes studied in the studio, and sketches of *fin-de-siècle* Paris streets, done with Marquet. In addition to these there are sculptures, engravings, aquatints and lithographs, book illustrations and paper cut-outs.

In Paris, the Musée National and the Musée Municipal d'Art Moderne are situated opposite each other in two wings of the same building, on the edge of the Seine. The first includes twenty-one paintings (*Luxury, Ill. 37, Odalisque with Red Trousers, Ill. 107, Decorative Figure on an Ornamental Background, Ill. 218, Buffet, Roumanian Blouse, Ill. 123, Still-life with a Magnolia, Two Friends, Ill. 132, Large Red Interior, Ill. 202*), three sculptures, a large gouache cut-out (*Sadness of the King, Ill. 135*), three tapestries and fifteen drawings. The second has as its prize *The Dance, Ill. 97*, the first version of the decoration intended for the Barnes Foundation, and three paintings, a sculpture and a drawing.

Matisse's engravings can be studied in the print room of the Bibliothèque Nationale (about a hundred and fifty works), as well as in the Bibliothèque Littéraire Jacques Doucet, in the Bibliothèque Sainte-Geneviève (about a hundred works, given by the artist with his valuable working copies of two illustrated books: *Pasiphaé*, *Ill. 151* and the *Lettres de la religieuse portugaise*, *Ill. 152*).

The route to follow from Paris to the Côte d'Azur must make an unexpected detour via Bordeaux, whose museum, thanks to Albert Marquet's widow, has acquired eight canvases originally owned by Matisse's close friend *(Belle–Ile, Spanish Girl)*. But Grenoble retains the distinction of having been the first French town to show an important collection of Matisse's work in a public exhibition, thanks to its enthusiastic curator Andry-Farcy. It actually consists of eight canvases, among which are *Still–life with a Red Carpet*, *Ill. 124*, the little *Pink Nude*, *Ill. 14*, and *Large Still–life with Aubergines*, *Ill. 201* (the latter a present from the artist's family, whereas the bulk comes from the Agutte-Sembat Collection), one sculpture and twenty-seven drawings.

Going down the Rhône Valley, a slight detour on the right bank before Avignon enables one to visit the museum of contemporary painting at Bagnols-sur-Cèze, whose often unexpected wealth owes nearly everything to the painter Albert André, a friend of Renoir. However the two Matisses it owns (a copy of Raphael's *Baldassare Castiglione*, *Ill. 23*, and a sparkling *View of Saint-Tropez*, *Ill. 29*) were both gifts from the government at the beginning of the century.

In Saint-Tropez itself the excellent Musée de l'Annonciade has five canvases (including the important *Gypsy*, *Ill. 220* of 1905) among the hundred odd modern works which perpetuate *in situ* the memory of the time when this resort— now a seaside extension of Saint-Germain-des-Prés—was a little fishing village, known only to a few painters.

Going from Saint-Tropez to Nice, one will naturally go to Vence to visit (Tuesday or Thursdays) the chapel of Notre-Dame du Rosaire, *Ills. 111–114*, bearing in mind Matisse's advice that 'the best season is winter' and 'the best hour, at that time, eleven o'clock in the morning', the moment when the stained glass windows receive the best light to 'show up the celestial prism'. In a corridor adjoining the chapel are thirty-four preparatory drawing for the *St Dominic*, the *Virgin* and the *Stations of the Cross* as well as a few lithographs.

Finally in Nice, last stage of the itinerary, the Musée Matisse was opened in January 1963 in the Villa des Arènes on the hill of Cimiez, very near the old Hôtel Régina where the painter had his home. Nowhere could be better chosen for the memorial than this calm and flowering garden, in the midst of such privileged nature and such a clear sky. Matisse's two sons and his daughter have faithfully carried out the wishes of their father (towards which he had made a gesture, while still alive, with his first gift to the town of Nice). This generous donation fills nine rooms and includes twenty canvases, eight sketches, five sculptures, five gouache cut-outs, one hundred and seventy drawings and one hundred and thirty-five engravings, together with the preliminary studies for Vence and a number of personal objects, all impeccably displayed.

The paintings can be split into two main groups, one dealing with the period 1890-8 (*Still-life with Books*, Ill. 16, *Still-life with White Candlestick*), the other with the collection that resulted from his stay in Nice (*Odalisque with Mimosa, Rough Armchair, Still-life with a Pomegranate*). An entire wall is covered with one of the largest gouache cut-outs: *Flowers and Fruit* (8.70×4.10 m). The very important collection of drawings includes, in particular, the series of preparatory drawings for *The Dance* at Merion, in which one can follow the origin and the development of the composition very clearly, from the initial realism through to the final solution.

The two rooms devoted to the development of the Vence Chapel contain two models, preparatory drawings, trial attempts for the windows and ceramics, and the admirable models of the vestments, in gouache cut-outs.

Finally one can examine pieces of furniture and familiar objects which featured so often in the artist's canvases and drawings, his collection of ceramics, bronzes, far-eastern paintings, Negro and Polynesian masks, as well as his palettes.

On leaving this moving collection, one goes very naturally to the master's grave, which is also that of his wife. It is situated low down in the cemetery at Cimiez, on a grassy terrace bordered with irises, shaded by olive trees, cypresses and eucalyptus. The memorial stone in white marble, without ornament, bears only the following inscription:

HENRI MATISSE
1869-1954

NOELLE MATISSE-PARAYRE
1872-1958

The itinerary above does not include some French towns whose museums own a few isolated works. These are: Albi (*Interior at Ciboure*), Céret (thirteen drawings), Lyon (*Portrait of M. Demotte*), Montélimar, Montpellier (*Still-life* and seven drawings), Nancy (*Seated Woman*), Reims (*Weaver*), Saint-Etienne (*Belle-Ile*), Saint-Nazaire (*Sea*).

One must obviously place the collections of Georges Duthuit and his wife (who was Marguerite Matisse) and Jean Matisse in the first rank of French private collections. Among the works most often reproduced are, from the former: *Interior with a Top Hat, Self-portrait 1900, Girl with a Black Cat, Marguerite Matisse, Ill. 49, Open Window*; from the latter; *Still-life with Books, Ill. 16, Port of Abaill, Collioure, Pont Saint-Michel, Self-portrait, 1918, Blue Table, Woman in a Blue Gandoura Dress*.

Among other notable French collections one can name those of Bernheim-Jeune, P. Berès (*Parakeet and Siren, Ill. 126*), H. Berggruen (*Black Door, Ill. 223*), J. Dubourg, K. Granoff, Maxime Blum, R. Hanert, G. Renand (*White Dress, Conversation, Ill. 183*), Niarchos (*Dinner Table, Ill. 8*), S. Bordat, Cuttoli, R. Hein, Ginette Signac (*Luxury, Calm and Delight, Ill. 32*) Pierre Lévy. Pablo Picasso owns, in particular, a portrait of *Marguerite, Ill. 39* and *Still-life with Oranges*, 1912, *Ill. 68*, one of the most accomplished of all.

One must put in a class by itself the critic George Besson's collection (which includes four of Matisse's paintings, of which two are portraits of Besson, and five drawings), object of a donation, subject to the donor's use during his lifetime, to the museums of Besançon and Bagnols-sur-Cèze, as well as the Jean Walter-Paul Guillaume collection, given under the same conditions to the national French museums by Mme Walter, which includes *Three Sisters* of 1917, plus nine canvases from the Nice period.

There are innumerable books, monographs, special numbers of reviews, articles and exhibition catalogues devoted to Matisse, dating from the first years of the century to the present day. Not only by specialists and art critics, but also by famous writers. Apollinaire, André Gide, Jules Romains, Montherlant, Aragon, Reverdy have contributed to this immense mass of material. Very complete bibliographies have been compiled on several occasions. The nature of the present volume forbids me to enumerate them, however summarily. But the reader who wants to deepen his knowledge of the artist has a right to a few references, which will enable him to go directly to the most important books.

While waiting for the complete catalogue of works, promised by Mme Marguerite Duthuit-Matisse, the basic reference book is still that of Alfred H. Barr Jr, Director of the New York Museum of Modern Art: *Matisse his Art and his Public* (New York, Museum of Modern Art, 1951), which follows period by period the painter's life and the development of all aspects of his work with unsurpassable historical and documentary precision, and is richly accompanied by illustrations, mainly in black and white.

Its equivalent in French is *Henri Matisse* by Gaston Diehl (Paris, Tisné, 1954), which, less concerned with exhaustive details, devotes more room to the study of the superior significance of the work and its importance in contemporary art. While the illustrations are less numerous they are of better quality and about half of them are in colour.

Jacques Lassaigne's monograph *Matisse* (Geneva, Skira, 1959) is concerned only with the painting and comments on it from the point of view of pure plastic art; its illustrations, all in colour, are good despite their small size. If one wishes to obtain a more varied view of the artist's personality and work, one can profitably read books by writers who knew him personally. Pierre Courthion's *Visage de Matisse* (Lausanne, Marquerat, 1943), *Matisse, ce vivant* by Raymond Escholier (Paris, Fayard, 1956), which include writings, extracts from letters and previously unpublished conversations. On the subject of his last period, at Vence and Nice, the testimonies of the poet André Verdet, *Prestiges de Matisse* (Paris, Emile Paul, 1952), and those of Père Couturier in his journal published under the title *Se garder libre* (Paris, Éditions du Cerf, 1962) present different aspects, if not opposite ones, of the story of the chapel at Vence.

No reader of French should deny himself the pleasure of reading the magnificent pages written by Aragon as an act of faith during the German occupation, under the title of *Matisse-en-France* (in *Matisse, Dessins, thèmes et variations,* Paris, Fabiani, 1943).

Les Fauves by Georges Duthuit, the artist's son–in–law, is a very brilliant essay written on a personal and emotional level, which shows the movement concentrated around its leader and compared with the most important movements in world art (Geneva, des Trois Collines, 1949). *Le Fauvisme* by Jean Leymarie (Geneva, Skira, 1959) is excellent as an objective study of historical and artistic facts, while *Les Fauves,* by J.–P. Crespelle (Neuchâtel, Ides et Calendes, 1962) evokes very clearly the atmosphere at the beginning of the century.

The drawings have been studied and reproduced separately, in particular by Waldemar George, Cl. Roger Marx, A. Humbert, M. Malingue and M. Valsecchi; the engravings by W.S. Liebermann: *Etchings by Matisse* (New York, Museum of Modern Art, 1955).

Of course, the files of the major artistic periodicals, mainly since the 1930s, contain a large number of important articles and valuable illustrations: *Formes, Cahiers d'Art, Verve, Le Point, XXe siècle, Art News Annual, La Biennale di Venezia* (special number in December 1955). To these one can add the album published by the University of California Press (texts by J. Leymarie, H. Read, W.S. Liebermann) on the occasion of the Matisse retrospective exhibition held in 1966 in Los Angeles (UCLA Art Galleries), Chicago (Art Institute), and Boston (Museum of Fine Arts).

On the chapel at Vence one can consult the July–August 1951 number of *L'Art Sacré,* as well as the study, in German, by G. Jedlicka *Die Matisse-Kapelle in Vence* (Frankfurt, 1955).

Lastly, the essence of Matisse's writings—he expressed himself with great precision and lucidity on the subject of his work throughout his entire life time—was been collected and edited by G. Diehl (*Notes d'un Peintre,* Paris, Hermann, 1967). H. Purrmann had previously edited another collection, in German, called *Farbe und Gleichnis* (Zurich, Verlag der Arche, 1955 and Frankfurt, Fischer, 1960). It only remains to hope that his most important letters, in particular those to André Rouveyre, will one day be published.

List of Illustrations

Index

1 *Self-portrait*, 1900. Brush drawing. Private collection.

2 *Carriage*, 1900. Brush drawing 22 × 33 cm. Musée du Cateau.

3 *Two Women in Town Clothes*, *c.* 1904. Dry-point 14.7 × 10 cm. Museum of Modern Art, New York.

4 Georges Antoine Rochegrosse: *The Death of Babylon*, 1891, Oil.

5 *White Feathers*, 1919. Oil 74 × 61 cm. Institute of Arts, Minneapolis.

6 Édouard Manet: *Portrait of Irma Brunner*, *c.* 1882. Oil 54 × 45 cm. Musée de l'Impressionnisme, Paris.

7 *Corsican Landscape*, 1898, Oil 38 × 46 cm. Musée de l'Annonciade, Saint-Tropez.

8 *Dinner Table*, 1897. Oil 100 × 131 cm. Niarchos collection, Paris.

9 *Landscape, Toulouse*, 1900. Oil 22 × 34 cm. Georges Renard collection, Paris.

10 Paul Cézanne: *Still-life*, *c.* 1890. Oil 65 × 81 cm. National Gallery of Art, Washington, D.C.

11 *Still-life with a Blue Patterned Tablecloth*, 1907. Oil 89 × 116 cm. Barnes Foundation, Merion, Pennsylvania.

12 *Notre-Dame in the Late Afternoon*, 1902. Oil 72 × 54 cm. Albright Art Gallery, Buffalo.

13 Paul Gauguin: *And the Gold of their Bodies*, 1901. Oil 67 × 76 cm. Musée de l'Impressionnisme, Paris.

14 *Pink Nude*, 1909. Oil 38 × 46 cm. Musée de Grenoble.

15 *View from my Window (Collioure)*, 1905. Pen drawing. Private collection.

16 *Still-life with Books*, 1890. Oil 38 × 46 cm. Private collection, Paris.

17 *Gustave Moreau's Studio*, 1895. Oil 65 × 81 cm. Private collection, Paris.

18 Gustave Moreau: *Autumn. C.* 1906. Watercolour 22 × 17 cm. Musée Gustave Moreau, Paris.

19 *Sleeping Nude*, *c.* 1906. Brush drawing 65 × 46 cm. Art Institute, Chicago.

20 Gustave Moreau: *Figures among Grottoes*, study for *Galatea*, *c.* 1880. Pencil drawing 32 × 21 cm. Musée Gustave Moreau, Paris.

21 *Nude* study for *The Joy of Living*, 1905. Ink drawing.

22 *Nude Study*, 1936. Pen drawing.

23 Copy by Matisse of *Baldassare Castiglione* by Raphael, *c.* 1894. Oil. Musée de Bagnols-sur-Cèze.

24 *Corsican Landscape*, 1898. Oil 38 × 46 cm. Musée des Beaux-Arts, Bordeaux.

25 *Pont Saint-Michel*, 1900. Oil 65 × 81 cm. William A. Burden collection, New York.

26 *Nude Study in Blue*, 1900. Oil 73 × 54 cm. Tate Gallery, London.

27 *Carmelina*, 1903. Oil 80 × 62 cm. Museum of Fine Arts, Boston.

28 *Lucien Guitry in the Role of Cyrano*, *c.* 1903. Oil 80.5 × 59.5 cm. William S. Paley collection, New York.

29 *View of Saint-Tropez*, 1904. Oil 35 × 48 cm. Musée de Bagnols-sur-Cèze.

30 *Woman in a Hat, Madame Matisse*, 1904-5. Oil 81 × 59.5 cm. Walter A. Haas collection, San Francisco.

31 Page from *l'Illustration* of 4 November 1905 showing fauve works in the Salon d'Automne of the year. Included are *Woman in a Hat (Ill. 30)* and *Open Window (Ill. 34)*.

32 *Luxury, Calm and Delight*, 1904-5. Oil 94 × 117 cm. Private collection, Paris.

33 *Pastorale*, 1905. Oil 46 × 55 cm. Musée du Petit Palais, Paris.

34 *Open Window, Collioure*, 1905. Oil 52,7 × 46 cm. John Hay Whitney collection, New York.

35 *Landscape, Collioure*, study for *The Joy of Living*, 1905. Oil 46 × 55 cm. Statens Museum for Kunst, Copenhagen.

36 *The Joy of Living*, 1905-6. Oil 174 × 238 cm. Barnes Foundation, Merion, Pennsylvania.

37 *Luxury*, 1907. Oil 210 × 138 cm. Musée National d'Art Moderne, Paris.

38 *Luxury II*, 1907-8. Oil 209,5 × 139 cm. Statens Museum for Kunst, Copenhagen.

39 *Marguerite*, 1906 or 1907. Oil. Pablo Picasso collection.

40 *Still-life with Asphodels*, 1907. Oil 115.5 × 89 cm. Folkwang Museum, Essen.

41 *La Coiffure*, 1907. Oil 116 × 89 cm. Staatsgalerie, Stuttgart.

42 *Bathers with a Tortoise*, 1908. Oil 184 × 220 cm. City Art Museum, Saint-Louis.

43 *Bowlers*, 1908. Oil 113,5 × 145 cm. State Hermitage Museum, Leningrad.

44 *Music*, 1907. Sketch 74 × 61 cm. Museum of Modern Art, New York.

45 *Bather*, 1909. Oil 92,7 × 74 cm. Museum of Modern Art, New York.

46 *Woman in Green*, 1909. Oil 65 × 54 cm. State Hermitage Museum, Leningrad.

47 *Algerian Woman*, 1909. Oil 80 × 65 cm. Musée National d'Art Moderne, Paris.

48 *Dinner-Table, Red Version*, 1908. Oil 181 × 220 cm. State Hermitage Museum, Leningrad.

49 *Girl with a Black Cat, Marguerite Matisse*, 1910. Oil 94 × 64 cm. Private collection, Paris.

50 *Madame Matisse with a Manila Shawl*, 1911. Oil 118 × 75 cm. R. Staechelin collection, Basle.

51 *The Dance*, 1910. Oil 260 × 391 cm. State Hermitage Museum, Leningrad.

52 Sketch for *The Dance*, 1909. Charcoal drawing. Musée de Grenoble.

53 *Music*, 1910. Oil 260 × 389 cm. State Hermitage Museum, Leningrad.

54 *Music (Second Stage)*, 1910. State Hermitage Museum, Leningrad.

55 *Blue Window*, 1911. Oil 130,8 × 90,5 cm. Museum of Modern Art, New York.

56 *Zorah Standing*, 1912. Oil 146,5 × 61 cm. State Pushkin Museum of Fine Arts, Moscow.

57 *Persian Miniature*, c. 1590. Fogg Art Museum, Cambridge, Massachusetts.

58 *Moroccan Landscape, Tangier*, 1911-12. Oil 115 × 80 cm. Nationalmuseum, Stockholm.

59 *Yellow Dress, Zorah*, 1912. Oil 81 × 64 cm. Alfred Cowles collection, Lake Forest, Illinois.

60 *Three Studies of Zorah*, 1912. Pen drawing 31 × 25 cm. Isabella Stewart Gardner Museum, Boston.

61 *Landscape seen through a Window*, *Tangier,* 1912. Oil 115 × 79 cm. State Pushkin Museum of Fine Arts, Moscow.

62 *Moroccan Woman*, 1911-12. Oil 36 × 28 cm. Musée de Grenoble.

63 *Seated Man of Rif*, 1913. Oil 200 × 160 cm. Barnes Foundation, Merion, Pennsylvania.

64 *Zorah on the Terrace*, 1912. Oil 115 × 100 cm. State Pushkin Museum of Fine Arts, Moscow.

65 *Madame Matisse*, 1913. Oil 146 × 97 cm. State Hermitage Museum, Leningrad.

66 *Woman on a Stool*, 1913-14. Oil 146 × 94 cm. Museum of Modern Art, New York.

67 *Goldfish*, 1915-16. Oil 146.5 × 112 cm. Museum of Modern Art, New York.

68 *Still-life with Oranges*, 1912. Oil 94 × 84 cm. Pablo Picasso collection.

69 *Goldfish*, 1911. Oil 147 × 98 cm. State Pushkin Museum of Fine Arts, Moscow.

70 *Bowl of Goldfish*, 1914. Oil 144 × 98 cm. Musée National d'Art Moderne, Paris.

71 *Studio, Quai Saint-Michel*, 1916. Oil 146 × 116.5 cm. Phillips collection, Washington.

72 *Moroccans*, 1916. Oil 181 × 280 cm. Museum of Modern Arts, New York.

73 *Piano Lesson*, 1916-17. Oil 245 × 213 cm. Museum of Modern Art, New York.

74 *Trees near the Trivaux Pond*, 1916. Oil 90.5 × 72.5 cm. Tate Gallery, London.

75 *Interior with Window*, 1916. Oil 146 × 116.5 cm. Institute of Arts, Detroit.

76 *Lorette in a Pink Armchair*, 1917. Oil 100 × 73 cm. H. Hahnloser collection, Berne.

77 *Green Dress. Lorette with a Black Background*, 1916. Oil 73 × 54 cm. Musée d'Art Moderne, Paris.

78 *Lorette*, 1916. Oil 55 × 46 cm. Ahrenberg collection, Stockholm.

79 *White Plumes*, 1919. Oil 78 × 60 cm. Göteborgs Konstmuseum, Gothenburg.

80 *White Plumes*, 1919. Pencil drawing. 37 × 24 cm. Museum of Art, Baltimore.

81 *White Plumes*, 1919. Pencil drawing. 52 × 35,3 cm. Institute of Arts, Detroit.

82 *White Plumes*, 1919. Ink drawing. 40 × 52 cm. Museum of Modern Art, New York.

83 *Venetian Blinds*, 1919. Oil 134 × 89 cm. Barnes Foundation, Merion, Pennsylvania.

84 *Black Table*, 1919. Oil 100 × 80.4 cm. H. Hahnloser collection, Berne.

85 *Artist and his Model*, 1919. Oil 60 × 73 cm. Harry Bakwin collection, New York.

86 *Artist among Olive Trees, c.* 1922. Oil 60 × 73 cm. Museum of Art, Baltimore.

87 *Seated Moorish Woman*, 1922. Oil 46 × 38 cm. Barnes Foundation Merion, Pennsylvania.

88 *Indian Trousers*, 1925. Lithograph. 54 × 43.5 cm. University of California, Los Angeles.

89 *Young Woman Painter*, 1923. Oil 73 × 63 cm. Mrs Maurice Newton collection, New York.

90 *Spaniard, Harmony in Blue, c.* 1923. Oil 47 × 28 cm. Lehman collection, New York.

91 *Odalisque*, 1923. Oil 61 × 74 cm. Stedelijk Museum, Amsterdam.

92 *Odalisque with Magnolias*, 1924. Oil 61 × 81 cm. Private collection, New York.

93 *Odalisque with a Green Scarf*, 1926. Oil 49 × 63 cm. Museum of Art, Baltimore.

94 *Odalisque with an Armchair*, 1928. Oil 60 × 73,5 cm. Petit Palais, Paris.

95 *Large Grey Nude*, 1929. Oil 105 × 82 cm. Private collection, Basle.

96 *Girl in Yellow*, 1929. Oil 100 × 81 cm. Museum of Art, Baltimore.

97 *The Dance (First Version)*, 1931-2. Oil 360 × 1.282 cm. Petit Palais, Paris.

98 *The Dance (Second Version)*, 1932-3. Oil 360 × 1434 cm. Barnes Foundation, Merion, Pennsylvania.

99 *Blue Eyes*, 1935. Oil 38 × 46 cm. Museum of Art, Baltimore.

100 *Pink Nude*, 1935. Oil 65 × 93 cm. Museum of Art, Baltimore.

101 *Hélène*, 1937. Oil 55 × 33 cm. Private collection.

102 *Mauve Dress*, 1937. Oil 73 × 60 cm. Museum of Art, Baltimore.

103 *France*, 1939. Oil 46 × 38 cm. Graindorge collection, Brussels.

104 *Conservatory*, 1937. Oil 72 × 60 cm. J. Pulitzer Jr collection, Saint-Louis.

105 *Music*, 1935. Oil 115 × 115 cm. Albright Art Gallery, Buffalo.

106 *Reader on a Black Background*, 1939. Oil 92 × 73 cm. Musée National d'Art Moderne, Paris.

107 *Odalisque with Red Trousers*, 1922. Oil 67 × 84 cm. Musée National d'Art Moderne, Paris.

108 *Odalisque with Mauve and White Striped Gown*, 1937. Oil 38 × 46 cm. Norton Simon collection, Los Angeles.

109 *Dancer*, 1938. Gouache cut-out, design for *l'Étrange Farandole*.

110 *Sword Swallower*, 1947. Gouache cut-out, illustration for *Jazz*.

111-114 Notre-Dame du Rosaire, Vence, 1947-51.

115 *Dreaming Woman in a Blouse*, 1936. Pen drawing.

116 Vincent van Gogh: *Schoolboy*, 1890. Oil 63 × 54 cm. Museu de Arte, São Paulo.

117 *Portrait with Green Streak*, 1905. Oil 40 × 32 cm. Statens Museum for Kunst, Copenhagen.

118-122 *Roumanian Blouse*, 1940. Preliminary studies.

123 *Roumanian Blouse*, 1940. Oil 92 × 72 cm. Musée National d'Art Moderne, Paris.

124 *Still-life with a Red Carpet*, 1906. Oil 89 × 116 cm. Musée des Beaux-Arts, Grenoble.

125 *Negress*, 1952-3. Gouache cut-out 160 × 625 cm. Private collection, Paris.

126 *Parakeet and Siren*, 1952. Gouache cut-out 327 × 773 cm. Private collection, Paris.

127 *Decorative Composition*, 1947. Gouache cut-out 51.5 × 217.5 cm. Kunstmuseum, Basle.

128 *Christmas Night*, 1951. Gouache cut-out, 335 × 135 cm. Maquette for a window for the *Time-Life* Building, New York. Museum of Modern Art, New York.

129–130 *Windows of Notre–Dame du Rosaire*, 1950. Gouache cut–out 465 × 200 cm. Maquettes for the second and third stages. Matisse family collection.

131 *Zulma*, 1950. Gouache cut–out 238 × 133 cm. Statens Museum for Kunst, Copenhagen.

132 *Two Friends*, 1941. Oil 61 × 50 cm. Museum of Modern Art, New York.

133–4 *Blue Nude III* and *Blue Nude IV*, 1952. Gouache cut–out 105 × 85 cm. 109 × 74 cm. Private collection, Paris.

135 *Sadness of the King*, 1952. Gouache cut–out 292 × 386 cm. Musée National d'Art Moderne, Paris.

136 *Negro Boxer*, 1947. Gouache cut–out. Musée National d'Art Moderne, Paris.

137 *Snail*, 1953. Gouache cut–out 286 × 287 cm. Tate Gallery, London.

138 *Nude, Head upside Down*, 1906. Lithograph 35.2 × 27.6 cm. Museum of Modern Art, New York.

139 *Landscape Seen through a Window, Tangier,* 1912. Ink drawing.

140 *Dancer and Armchair, Black Background*, 1942. Oil 50 × 64 cm. Mrs Marcel Duchamp collection, New York.

141 *Woman Playing a Guitar*, 1939. Charcoal drawing. Private collection, Paris.

142 *Nude Study*, 1936. Pen drawing. Private collection, New York.

143 *Siesta*, 1937. Lino–cut 26 × 32 cm. University of California, Los Angeles.

144 *Beautiful Tahitian*, 1937. Lino–cut 28 × 19,5 cm. University of California, Los Angeles.

145 *White Frill*, 1936. Pen drawing. 38 × 28 cm. Museum of Art, Baltimore.

146 *Nude in the Studio*, 1935. Pen drawing. Private collection, New York.

147 *Still–life with Fruit and a Cup of Coffee*, 1941. Pen drawing. Private collection.

148 *Nude with Black Ferns*, 1948. Brush drawing 105 × 75 cm. Musée National d'Art Moderne, Paris.

149 *Dahlias and Pomegranates*, 1947. Brush drawing 72 × 56,5 cm. Museum of Modern Art, New York.

150 Illustration from *Poésies* by Stéphane Mallarmé (Lausanne, Skira, 1932). Etching. Page size 33 × 25 cm.

151 Illustration from *Pasiphaé* by Henry de Montherlant (Paris, Fabiani, 1944). Lino–cut. Page size 32.5 × 24.5 cm.

152 Two pages from *Lettres de la Religieuse portugaise* (Paris, Tériade, 1946). Lithograph. Page size 27.8 × 20.5 cm.

153 Study of *Marianna Alcoforado* for *Lettres de la Religieuse portugaise*, 1945. Charcoal drawing. Musée Municipal, Cambrai.

154 Illustration from *Les Fleurs du Mal* by Baudelaire (Paris, La Bibliothèque Française, 1947). Lithograph. Page size 28 × 23 cm.

155 Two pages from *Florilège des Amours* by Ronsard (Paris, Skira, 1948). Lithograph. Page size 38 × 28 cm.

156 Frontispiece and Title–page from *Poèmes de Charles d'Orléans* (Paris, Tériade, 1950). Coloured lithograph. Page size 42 × 26.5 cm.

157 *The Slave*, 1902-1903. Bronze Museum of Art, Baltimore.

158 Auguste Rodin: *Walking Man*, 1877. Bronze 225 cm. high. Musée Rodin, Paris.

159 *Madeleine I*, 1901. Bronze 60 cm. high. Museum of Art, Baltimore.

160 *Reclining Nude I*, 1907. Bronze. 34.4 cm. high, 49.2 cm. long. Musée National d'Art Moderne, Paris.

161 *Blue Nude (Souvenir de Biskra)*, 1907. Oil 92 × 140 cm. Museum of Art, Baltimore.

162 *Sculpture and Goldfish*, 1911. Oil 116 × 100 cm. John Hay Whitney collection, New York.

163 *Two Negresses*, 1908. Bronze 47 cm. high. Museum of Art, Baltimore.

164 *Serpentine*, 1909. Bronze 56 cm. high. Statens Museum for Kunst, Copenhagen.

165 Gallo-Roman: *Nude Woman*. Bronze 14 cm. high. Musée historique de l'Orléanais, Orléans.

166 *Interior with a Violin*, 1917. Oil 116 × 89 cm. Statens Museum for Kunst, Copenhagen.

167 *Mauve Dress*, 1942. Oil 55 × 38 cm. Léon Duesberg collection, Soiron-Verviers, Belgium.

168 *Jeannette I*, 1910. Bronze 31 cm. high. Museum of Modern Art, New York.

169 *Jeannette II*, 1910. Bronze 26.6 cm. high. Museum of Modern Art, New York.

170 *Jeannette III*, 1910-11. Bronze 61 cm. high. Museum of Modern Art, New York.

171 *Jeannette IV*, 1910-11. Bronze 62.5 cm. high. Museum of Modern Art, New York.

172 *Jeannette V*, 1910-11. Bronze 57.9 cm. high. Museum of Modern Art, New York.

173 *Still-life with Oysters*, 1940. Oil 65.5 × 81.5 cm. Kunstmuseum, Basle.

174 *Pineapples and Anemones*, 1940. Oil 73 × 92 cm. Mrs Albert D. Lasker collection, New York.

175 *Reclining Nude II*, c. 1929. Bronze. 18 cm. high. Museum of Art, Baltimore.

176 *Seated Nude*, 1925. Bronze 78 cm. high. Private collection, Paris.

177 *The Back I*, c. 1910. Bronze 187 × 115.6 cm. Tate Gallery, London.

178 *The Back II*, c. 1913. Bronze 186.6 × 115.5 cm. Tate Gallery, London.

179 *The Back III*, c. 1916-17. Bronze 185.3 × 113.9 cm. Tate Gallery, London.

180 *The Back IV*, c. 1930. Bronze 186 × 114 cm. Tate Gallery, London.

181 *Nude Study*. Charcoal drawing 46 × 25 cm. Mme Hazan collection, Paris.

182 *Idol*, 1942. Oil 71 × 92 cm. Mrs Albert D. Lasker collection, New York.

183 *Conversation*, 1941. Oil 65 × 54 cm. Private collection, Paris.

184 *Persian Woman*, 1929. Lithograph 43 × 28 cm. University of California, Los Angeles.

185 *Nude Upside Down*, 1935. Pen drawing.

186 *Dancer Sitting in an Armchair*, 1942. Oil 33 × 46 cm. Private collection, Paris.

187 *Dancer in a Blue Tutu*, 1942. Oil 46 × 38 cm. Private collection, Paris.

188 *The Reader, Marguerite Matisse*, 1906. Oil 64 × 90 cm. Musée des Beaux-Arts, Grenoble.

189 *Marguerite Reading, c.* 1906. Pen drawing 29.6 × 52 cm. Museum of Modern Art, New York.

190 *Madame Matisse in Red Madras*, 1907-8. Oil 99 × 80 cm. Barnes Foundation, Merion, Pennsylvania.

191 *Portrait of Serge Shchukin*, 1912. Charcoal drawing 47 × 32 cm. Pierre Matisse collection, New York.

192 *Portrait of Sarah Stein*, 1916. Oil 73 × 56 cm. Museum of Art, San Francisco.

193 *Portrait of Claribel Cone*, 1933. Charcoal drawing 59 × 40.5 cm. Museum of Art, Baltimore.

194 *Self-portrait with a Straw Hat*, 1941. Red chalk 48 × 37 cm. Musée du Cateau.

195 *Portrait of Cortot*, 1926. Drypoint 14.3 × 7.3 cm. University of California, Los Angeles.

196 *Michaela*, 1943. Oil 58 × 71 cm. Mrs Maurice Newton collection, New York.

197 *Seated Odalisque*, 1928. Oil 55 × 38 cm. Museum of Art, Baltimore.

198 *Tahitian Landscape*, 1930. Pen drawing.

199 *Rocking-chair, Tahiti*, 1930. Pen drawing.

200 *Red Studio*, 1911. Oil 181 × 219 cm. Museum of Modern Art, New York.

201 *Large Still-life with Aubergines*, 1911-12. Oil 210 × 244.3 cm. Musée des Beaux-Arts, Grenoble.

202 *Large Red Interior*, 1948. Oil 146 × 97 cm. Musée National d'Art Moderne, Paris.

203 *Large Interior, Nice*, 1921. Oil 132 × 89 cm. Art Institute, Chicago.

204 *Woman on a Divan*, 1922. Oil 60 × 73.5 cm. Kunstmuseum, Basle.

205 *Asia*, 1946. Oil 116 × 81 cm. Tom May collection, Beverly Hills, California.

206 *Interior with an Egyptian Curtain*, 1948. Oil 116 × 89 cm. Phillips collection, Washington.

207 *Gourds*, 1916. Oil 65 × 81 cm. Museum of Modern Art, New York.

208 *Pewter Jug*, 1916-17. Oil 92 × 65 cm. Museum of Modern Art, Baltimore.

209 *Tulips and Oysters*, 1943. Oil 60 × 73 cm. Pablo Picasso collection.

210 *Lemons and Pewter Jug*, 1939. Oil 55 × 46 cm. Pétridès collection, Paris.

211 *Lemons and Mimosa on Black Background*, 1944. Oil 64 × 73 cm. Private collection.

212 *Still-life*, 1946. Oil 92 × 65 cm. Musées Royaux de Belgique, Brussels.

213 *Music Lesson*, 1917. Oil 244 × 210 cm. Barnes Foundation, Merion, Pennsylvania.

214 *Piano Lesson*, 1923. Oil 64 × 81 cm. Royan Middleton collection, Dundee.

215 *Nude with an Empire Necklace*, 1936. Oil. Private collection, Paris.

216 *Nude by a Mirror*, 1937. Pen drawing. Private collection, Paris.

217 *Moorish Screen*, 1922. Oil 92 × 74 cm. Museum of Art, Philadelphia.

218 *Decorative Figure on an Ornamental Background*, 1927. Oil 130 × 98 cm. Musée National d'Art Moderne, Paris.

219 *Kneeling Nude*, 1950. Charcoal drawing. Aimé Maeght collection, Paris.

220 *Gypsy*, 1906. Oil 55 × 46 cm. Musée de l'Annonciade, Saint-Tropez.

221 *The fifth Station of the Cross*, Notre-Dame du Rosaire, Vence, 1947–51.

222 *Portrait of a Woman*, 1944. Pen drawing.

223 *Black Door*, 1942. Oil 61 × 38 cm. Heinz Berggruen collection, Paris.

224 *The Lived-in Silence of Houses*, 1947. Oil 61 × 50 cm. Private collection, Paris.

225 *Hindu Pose*, 1923. Oil 72 × 59.5 cm. Donald Stralem collection, New York.

226 *Young English Girl*, 1947. Oil 55 × 33 cm. Private collection, Paris.

227 *Sleeping Woman*, 1936. Pen drawing.

228 Illustration for *Poésies* by Mallarmé (Lausanne, Skira, 1932).

229 Pablo Picasso: *Head of a Girl*.

230 *Nude Study*, 1936. Pen drawing.

231 *Woman with a Bouquet of flowers*, 1940. Pen drawing.

Index

ALCOFORADO, Marianna, 163, *153*
ARAGON, Louis, 189, 211, 241
ARMORY SHOW, The, 226

BARNES, Dr, 98, 232, 233
BARR, Alfred H. Jr, 240
BARYE, Antoine-Louis, 44, 165
BAUDELAIRE, Charles, 52, 112, *154*
BAZAINE, Jean, 214, 228
Blaue Reiter, Der, 226
BONNARD, Pierre, 26, 39, 92, 222
BRAQUE, Georges, 139
Brücke, Die, 225

CAMPAUX, François, 114, 150
CAPELLADES, Père, 122
CÉZANNE, Paul, 19, 20, 21, 27, 32, 42, 50, *10*
CONE, Claribel, 54, *193*
CONE, Etta, 231
CORTOT, *195*
COURTHION, Pierre, 48, 76, 98, 103, 168, 240
COUTURIER, Père, 117, 119, 121, 214, 216, 240
CUBISM, 82, 83, 226

DEGAS, Edgar, 184
DELAUNAY, Robert, 226
DELEKTORSKAYA, Lydia, 114
DERAIN, André, 41, 48, 50, 53, 189
DIAGHILEV, Serge, 110
DIEHL, Gaston, 76, 77, 240
DIVISIONISM, *see* neo-impressionism
DURAND-RUEL, 18, 26, 28
DUTHUIT, Georges, 51, 112, 241

EHRENBURG, Ilya, 189
ESCHOLIER, Raymond, 51, 240

FAUVISM, 49–53

GAUGUIN, Paul, 22, 23, 27, 50, *13*
GUITRY, Lucien, *28*

HUYGHE, René, 135

IMPRESSIONISM, 18, 19

JOYCE, James, 111

KANDINSKY, Wassily, 226
KIRCHNER, Ernst Ludwig, 225

LASSAIGNE, Jacques, 240
LÉGER, Fernand, 226

MAILLOL, Auguste, 179
MALLARMÉ, Stéphane, 111, 159, *150*, *228*
MANET, Édouard, 18, *6*
MARQUET, Albert, 33, 40, 41, 70, 86, 157, 189, 195
MASSINE, Léonide, 110
MATISSE, Mme, 70, 128, 130, 189, *30*, *50*, *65*, *117*, *190*
MATISSE, Marguerite, 70, 189, *49*, *188*, *189*
MONET, Claude, 18, 19
MONTHERLANT, Henry de, 111, 159, 189, *151*
MOREAU, Gustave, 25, 26, 35, 36, 37, 38, 41, *18*, *20*
MOROZOV, Ivan, 54, 234

NABIS, 26, 27, 28, 35
Neo-impressionism, 19, 45, 46

ORLÉANS, Charles d', 112, 163, 164, *156*

PICASSO, Pablo, 82, 97, 114, 139, 178, 227, *229*
PROKOFIEV, Sergei, 189
PUY, Jean, 41

RAYSSIGUER, Frère, 115
REDON, Odilon, 25
RENOIR, Auguste, 18, 92, 184, 215
REVERDY, Pierre, 111
ROCHEGROSSE, Georges-Antoine, *4*
RODIN, Auguste, 44, 165, 167, *158*

Ronsard, 112, 163, *155*
Rothko, Mark, 227
Rouault, Georges, 35, 36, 214
Rouveyre, André, 112, 198, 241

Seurat, Georges, 19
Shchukin, Serge, 54, 61, 65, 234, *191*
Shostakovich, Dmitri, 110
Signac, Paul, 19, 135
Stein family, 54, 231, *192*
Stieglitz, Alfred, 226

Stravinsky, Igor, 110
Symbolism, 23, 25

Turner, Joseph Mallord, 40

Van Gogh, Vincent, 21, 22, 27, 42, 127, 128, *116*
Vauxcelles, Louis, 49
Verdet, André, 124, 146, 217, 240
Vlaminck, Maurice, 42, 50, 53
Vollard, Ambroise, 20, 28, 42, 54
Vuillard, Édouard, 26, 39, 48